To Aunt Agnes

Pamela Thompson

Time To Remember

by
Pamela Thompson

authorHOUSE®

AuthorHouse™ UK Ltd.
500 Avebury Boulevard
Central Milton Keynes, MK9 2BE
www.authorhouse.co.uk
Phone: 08001974150

© 2007 Pamela Thompson. All rights reserved.

No part of this book may be reproduced, stored in a retrieval system, or transmitted by any means without the written permission of the author.

First published by AuthorHouse 11/8/2007

ISBN: 978-1-4343-4038-2 (sc)

Printed in the United States of America
Bloomington, Indiana

This book is printed on acid-free paper.

I would like to dedicate this book to my Grandson Andrew. Through his questions over the years he has wanted to know about the war. I did some notes which Joanne and Michelle and other people saw. They have encouraged me to write "Time to Remember".

The two ladies who look after me have become good friends to me who I have grown very fond of. They have also inspired me when they read my notes. They have been coming to me for years. Thank you Joanne who comes to sort my hair out and Michelle my home help who comes to sort my mess out.

Chapter One
PRE WAR

7th June 1937 today was the day that the last twinkle in my Dad's eye was born.

Mum used to say that I was a should not have been, and the last twinkle in my Dads eye.

Dad was 46 and Mum was 42. Both Mum and my sister were named Edith and Dad and my brother were both Edwin.

For recognition I will refer to mum as mum, sister Ede my father Dad and Brother Ted.

Ede was 14 and Ted 18 when I was born, taking this into consideration no wonder I was a should not have been.

Many people thought Ede was my Mum, and that Mum was my Gran. Even now people still think this.

Mum told me they had a problem in that they could not decide what to call me - Pat, Pauline, Paula, Pest or Pamela.

Pamela Thompson

The latter won!

I think she was kidding me about the name pest because how did they know what I would be like in the future?

My mum had been in Davyhulme Hospital for 2 weeks and as usual I created a problem.

When I was born my weight was just less than 2 lbs, my mum had quite a bad time due to her age.

My problem was rare, the afterbirth came first then me, also I was delivered with forceps which created a cut at the top of my head, this has stayed with me to this day.

I remember at the age of about 6 I found a little bare spot on my head measuring roughly about quarter of an inch.
I cried and cried I thought I was going bald.

Mum explained to me what had happened.

I apparently spent 6 weeks in hospital due to my weight and cut head.

Up to the age of 6 or 7all my memories are flashes which come back from time to time.

From the end of the war my memories are memories, not just flash backs.

On questioning my parents about these flashes they told me what they were connected to.

I think these flashes were caused by being frightened and scared at certain events at the time.

Chapter Two
WAR YEARS

On 3rd Sept 1939 Britain, France, Australia and New Zealand declared war on Germany.

One of the main reasons being the invasion of Poland.

This news was given to us by the radio. Everybody was aware that this may happen.

During this time people were hoping that the problem Germany had with Poland would go away, but as we all know it did not.

Germany invaded Poland on the 1st September 1939.
From this time on most of the world felt the occupation,
Of their country, Hungary was the last.

March 1944. Italy and Russia were fighting with Germany, later they came over to our side.

Up to the age of about 3 we lived in South Avenue, Davyhulme, Eccles.

Time To Remember

About 1940 my mum bought my aunties sweet shop on Brindleheath Road, Salford.

A lot of my recollections come from this time.

I remember the shed in the whitewashed back yard at the shop where my father bred budgerigars and canaries, little tiny featherless, bare and skinny they were so small I could hold four in one hand.

The toilet was also in the yard, you would freeze if you did not put on your coat, scarf and gloves.

In those days there were no such things as toilet rolls. Dad had Ede and I cutting up squares of newspapers and threading string through the hole we made in the top corner to hang them up (guess where) yes the toilet; the print from the paper gave you a nice black bum!!

The problem with the toilet being outside was in the winter they became frozen.

A solution to this was a Kelly Lamp, even though it was only approx 5" high it did do its job to stop the toilet from freezing. It also gave a bit of light to the users.

The lamp was run on paraffin which was not very nice to inhale. Black sooty fumes they made you cough and splutter, not nice at all.

Eventually when you could not buy candles, the Kelly Lamp took over.

Everybody found some use for the Kelly Lamp. We used ours during the black outs, the black outs were very serious.

Black sheets or a dark colour had to be put up to the windows. Anything to block out any light.

If light was showing there would be a loud banging on the door. The warden would shout in no uncertain manner "Put that light out ""Put that light out".

Apparently even somebody striking a match would show as a bright light in the sky.

Before we could go to bed we had to put siren suits, gas masks, a strong pair of shoes and a blanket at the end of the bed, pick up the money and important documents, and put the shutters up at the shop.

This happened every night, and then off to the shelter.

I remember the stoning of all steps 4 in the yard, 2 at the shop front. They were kept clean with Donkey Stones, where they got the name from I do not know. These stones were, brown, cream or white. The step was wet and the stone was put on in either a pattern or all over. Then with a very damp cloth the

stoning was made smooth. This was how all steps were cleaned at that time. We acquired our stones mainly from the rag and bone man.
If you took him old rags etc he would give you a balloon, kite, little toy, book, windmill or a stone. These stones lasted ages and ages.

We looked forward to the Rag and Bone man coming, to see what we would get. We would also have a little chat to the donkey that pulled his cart?

When what we called Red Raddel came out stoning the steps became a thing of the past.

The yard was whitewashed at least once a year it was a messy job.
Dad had blotches of white wash all over him.

My Dad was a very quiet man never wanting to go out, my sister and brother both had this trait not like mum and I. We would go anywhere at any time until she almost became housebound with Rheumatoid Arthritis.

My Mum had an Aunty who we knew lived near where the Brabazon aircraft was being built in Weston-super-mare. But we did not realise just how near she lived.

When aunt's daughter Joy became very ill mum and I decided to go and see her. Even though we were at war you could travel, the trains were running but at reduced time table. This turn out to be a very eventful trip.

Mums Aunty lived near the airfield in fact the road she lived on had houses built one side of the road only. Opposite was the Airfield.

I remember being very frightened when we had an Air Raid. Some went in the Toilet for safety, others under the stairs. These places were supposed to be the safest.

Mum and I hid under the table in the living room which had a large window looking over the airfield. I have seen a sight which I hope I will never see again. The utter fright of seeing an enemy Aircraft flying over the house pulling up high after flying low over the airfield dropping its bombs. I was petrified as the aircraft was still low going over the houses. I could see the figure of the pilot as he was trying to pull back to clear the houses. The noise and the aircraft trying not to hit the houses were awful. It was a sight I will never forget.

Mum and I were going home the following day, but were told that the railway station had taken a direct hit. We had to stay an extra 3 days, and go from a station 10 miles away. We were taken by car to the station by a friend of my Aunts. After changing trains 3 times we eventually got home.

Mum also had a friend Maud who lived in Prestatyn

Time To Remember

Wales - They met in Southamton where they were both nurses, in World War 1.

Ede, Mum and I went to see her quite a lot. It was on one of these trips that my sister met Harry her future husband. He had come over from Italy where he was a Red Cap. His home town was Romford Essex.

My sister's friend Flo was with us on this holiday, they both met Harry and his friend Bob. Unfortunately Bob was killed when they went back to Italy.

Wales was inundated with lots of Americans, waiting to invade Germany, they were housed in Hotels, Flats etc.

As all the other Seaside Resorts, Wales Beaches had been mined and a lot of areas had been camouflaged to stop the invaders from landing.

There were also a number of hospitals which were taken over for the use of troupes who had lost limbs, and needed a lot of nursing. My Mum had experience nursing amputees and soldiers who had been badly wounded in the 1st World War. Maud was already nursing at one of the hospitals.

When just Mum and I were on a visit, an extra large amount of casualties arrived who were very badly wounded. Mum decided she would stay and do

what was needed and sent for Ede to come and take me home.
Mrs Simcox helped Ede and Dad with the shop and mum stayed for 4 weeks.

People would ask mum what the difference was, nursing in World War 1 and 2. Mum used to say that the smallest of things like instead of having to cut bandages from old blankets or any kind of materials which had been boiled, it was good to have them ready, saving a lot of time.

Dad worked in the shop; he also drove a public tram. When the change came from trams to buses he decided he wanted to work in the bus depot where he stayed till he retired.

He was in the veterinary core during the First World War in Gallipoli. The stories he could tell were amazing.

He told Ede and I what had happened to his shoulder. He could push a knitting needle in the dent, it almost went through to the other side. When he was in Gallipoli his unit was being over run with the enemy, he was giving his officer his horse when a shot rang out, the officer was stood at the back of my dad, the bullet went through his right shoulder and straight into the officer's stomach and killed him.

When all the soldiers were coming home on Boats, Dads ship was torpedoed -yes torpedoed, the first!

Time To Remember

The first were just about manufactured towards the end of War 1 in 1918.

In those days compared with today, the latest thing in warfare was not very accurate but never the less they sank my Dads ship. He had very strong memories about swimming in the Aegean Sea.

The possibility of drowning was not the only thing to be scared of. It was all the debris floating about from other torpedoed ships. It put many soldiers including my Dad in hospital for months recovering from the wounds caused by debris.

In our home we had many pieces of embroidery, all beautifully done, it always fascinated me, head protectors for sofas and chairs, tea cosies etc and knitted items, and the embroidery was outstanding. I found out that my Dad had done them while he was recovering in hospital after the sinking.

They had teachers in the hospitals to help with the rehabilitation programs which included embroidery and knitting; This is where he got the skill.

He spent hours teaching me how to embroider at the end I was quite good at it, but not as good as Dad.

Before he went into the Army he was a good tennis player, when he came home his legs were better but he could not play anymore.

The 1st world war ended on 11th November 1918, when Germany signed an armistice with the Allies.

This is why we have the 11th November every year to remember the dead of both 1 and 2 wars. The saying "Never have so few given so much to so many" (Well done Winston Churchill) I can not think of any words to equal this phrase it is so true. This is indeed a thank you to the men and women who gave their lives for us.

My sister worked in a grocery shop until she had to do munitions work when the second war broke out? Mum who was a nurse in the First World War looks after the shop.

I knew I had a brother but I had no recollections of him at all, he was in World War 2 and served almost 5 years in Burma.

My first memories of the war in about 1942 were the air raid sirens, everybody immediately got up and put on their siren suit which were at the ready at the bottom of the bed. They were like today's baby grows in a warm material, pick up our gas mask and rush off to the Air raid shelter. There were various shelters which had been organised by the council.

Ours were built under the railway bridges that they blocked up at each end they put in bunk beds, furnished with black paraffin heaters (you know what I think about them).

The children got in the bunks and waited for Mrs Simcox to come round with the coco it was a great treat for us all but it tasted horrible Mrs S boiled water on the black stove added the coco, no milk or powdered milk and no sugar.
I do not know how we drank it, at the time it was a great treat. If we were lucky we might get a home made biscuit which were made by various people, if they could get the flour etc.

Coco became the children's substitute for sweets and chocolate. Your mum would put coco powder and sugar mixed together in a paper and off you would go dipping your finger in and suck it off that became our nearest thing to chocolate.

Mrs Simcox became a good friend when Mums legs became very bad.
Mrs S came to do some of the house work and many other things to help..

In the Air Raid shelter there was a large bucket with a handle. This was for children and ladies only in case they needed to go urgently. The men also used it sometimes when they were desperate. This bucket was positioned near the Exit to the shelter. This was not hygienic but it was readily accepted.

There was always somebody who would moan and grown about the facilities we had, until they heard the circumstances other people had to live with.

There were all kinds of shelters put up, people with gardens would dig quite a big hole, put some kind of corrugated Iron roof on.

My friend had one of these which she hated. When it rained it made a loud sound, and frightened her, not to mention they all sat with umbrellas up, it rained in so hard.
It was said that the safest place to go was either under the stairs or in the cellar. Quite often people stayed in the house as normal.

After seeing later how the people in London, used the underground as a shelter, packed in like sardines, trying to sleep nearly one on top of the other and lying on newspapers, try to make a drink on a little Burner, it made me realise that our shelter was not that bad. At least we could make a drink and had a Bunk, and room to walk about, not an ideal situation but under the circumstances we did not do too badly.

The most frightening were the doodle bug bombs. They made an awful screaming sound when the screaming stopped there would be a minute's silence, then you heard the bomb explode.

There was silence in the shelter, every body held their breath until the bomb exploded keeping our fingers crossed that it was not our shelter that got bombed.

The men on ARP duty including Dad would run round all the shelters, report any damage, control the blackouts, get the injured off to hospital and sort other problems. They wore a Helmet with a W on it.

I believe there was somewhere about one and half million on ARP duties around the country. At the end of each Raid they went round the shelters to see if we were all OK, then went on with their duties.

The All Clear siren was an anxious time, nobody knew if they had a home to go to or would have to go back to the shelter.

I remember one night after an air raid we got back to the shop to find the whole of the large window was just a few shards of glass and wood.

When we closed the shop at night, four large strong shutters were put up to the windows, an Iron Bar went across the shutters with 2 large padlocks one at each end. The iron bar and the padlocks were never seen again. I remember trying to find them.

Opposite the shop was St Ann's School, all the windows had been blown out.

We found out later that the caretaker who was in the school had been killed, we never found out what had killed him. There were no bombs dropped on

the school so it was not a bomb that killed him. Everything was shattered but no bombs.
They had a direct hit on the bank on the junction of Brindleheath Road and Broad St. Also the first six houses at the top of Brindleheath had gone with the bank.

The Council soon had this sight cleared and built a British Restaurant. These were built all over the country, they were for anybody who wanted a hot meal which cost about 6p. These constructions remained for quite a few years after the war.

The Barrage balloons were still there, there were 8 most of the time. They were there to protect the railway sidings from bombing. They had gun powder, grenades, guns and all kinds of munitions waiting to be despatched.

I have often thought what a stupid place to put our Air Raid shelters...
Under the railway bridges leading to the sidings where munitions were stored.

We did experience more raids in this area because of the railway being one of the targets for bombing.

The next day it was realised that we had been in the Blitz which started Sept 1940 and ended May 1941. The whole of Britain was bombed by the Luftwaffe night and day. London and Coventry, were almost wiped out they had continual bombing night and day.

The worst of the Bombing had yet to come the "Rockets" London was bombarded with the V2 Rockets, which left London almost flattened.

During all this I used to drive my Mum mad. I lived opposite to St Ann's School, I do not remember any of the following. Apparently I kept sneaking out of school, and hiding in the cellar at the shop. I got so bad I was taken from St Ann's and sent to Halton Bank which was quite a walk. I did run away quite a few times, but found it too far to run home.

Eventually I did settle down. I remained at Halton Bank till I left at 15. Only the other day while watching TV about nitty heads, I remember the nit nurse coming. If there was a problem found, you were sent home with a note advising what should be done.

No such things as creams and shampoos in those days. The main thing was a nit comb with very narrow teeth made of steel. This was dragged through your hair, dragging clumps of hair out as well as nits and eggs.

We were visited by various nurses for general medicals, eye tests etc.

They even measured us for coupons for shoes if

needed. I tried my best to get coupons for shoes. The nurse would draw a line from the wall, to cover size 5 shoes for the girls. I remember standing there trying to stretch my feet over the line but never made it.

Halton Bank was a boys and girl's school mixed classes we had our own play yards. I remember one day the boys let the bees out from there hives which were on the border of the boys and girls yards. They caused mayhem in the girl's yard as they escaped our way. After that they were housed at the furthest place from the girl's yard as possible. To our amazement nobody was stung.

I enjoyed school, even though I was not the brightest spark in the class. I was the only one who got <u>minus</u> 10 Out of 20 for spelling. My teacher used to hold his head in despair with my spelling. I put an e at the end of everything, come was cume.

I hated English classes, but give me a set of account books to balance, no problem. Top of the Maths Class, bottom of English class.

My sewing Teacher also had a problem with me, I remember when we were taught French seams we were making P.E shorts. They ended up as shorts for my doll, but my embroidery was displayed on the wall.

I enjoyed Miss Rogers dancing class, quick steps

waltz etc. I just had one problem I was tall, when we were short on boys I had to be the man. For those who were confused with which way they should be going and the steps, she made 2 sets of footprints, one for the girls and one for the boys. Black for the boys and white for the girls she set them out on the floor, showing which way to go.

When I was older knowing the mens steps was sometimes an advantage.
Much later it caused me a big problem. The excuses the boys came up with when they did not attend lessons, were nearly always the same they had hurt their leg. One excuse was "His Shoes Were to Tight".

My favourite was making things for the War Effort. Mum did a lot for the war efforts; this kept me busy and a few school friends.

We collected shoe boxes or any other type of box these were filled with things like razor blades, tooth paste, sewing needles, cotton, tape, soap, plasters, tablets like Asprin,
Pens, pencils, cigarettes when my mum could get them. All types of things what ever you could get in the boxes.

Then there were the slippers, I wish I had a ld for all The slippers I have knitted.

It was surprising how many felt hats we collected,

Pamela Thompson

every body had the old felt hats. These hats made good soles for the slippers which were sent to the field hospitals for patients to rest their feet.

We cut out a sole, knitted a piece to make the back and side, then knitted a top which was more or less a triangle, then stitch the back and triangle, to the felt, then make a lace to keep them on.

This was done by a cotton reel, in those days the reels were made of wood.
Today they are plastic, 4 tacks would be knocked into the top of the real, then put the end of the wool through the centre of the real then the wool was wound round the tacks three times.

The bottom one would be pulled over each tack, and wrap the wool round once till the lace you wanted was long enough. As you took the wool over, pull the bottom down. Continue doing this until the lace is long enough.

In those days there was no such thing as double knitting wool. If you only had thin wool we used to knit with two or three strands of wool for the slipper.

As well as going round collecting old felt we also collected old wool, some times the slippers would be 5 or 6 different colours, depending what we could get.

Time To Remember

Besides going round collecting, my school and all the shops around had large boxes for people to put anything in. Things were made for soldiers and evacuated children.

Every thing we made was collected from a school. Sometimes there were notes inside for the person receiving it. We never knew who would get what, on some occasions a letter would come from someone who had received a parcel.

The children who had been evacuated got, comics, books, crayons, toys, anything that people gave to us. This was a time when the camaraderie was at its highest. Every body had time for each other, helping as much as possible.
It was also a time when what was called "Black Market" this came about when people would trade with each other especially shop keepers.

They all knew somebody who had got something for sale at a price, or doing swaps.

The lady who had the grocers up the road used to make Ham and Pea soup and sell it by the basin full. She would keep part of the orders that came in till she had enough to make this soup, it was very nice. Sometimes she would swap mum a ham shank for sweets. This is how I got my liking for pea and ham soup.

From the butcher she would do a swap for a couple

of sausages. Every thing was on ration we each had a Ration Book which had various coupons in for everything from meat to cloths.

It was quite a job counting all the coupons and send them to the food office.
An E was a quarter pound of sweets, and 2ozs for a D.

You could spend them at any time in any shop, when you could find a shop with sweets. When they had gone that was it, no more till next month. The coupons were sent out in months or weeks.

At the beginning of Rationing the Government made certain provision for children under 2 received free cod-liver oil, Blackcurrant and orange juice.

School children were allowed one third of a pint of milk free. This was given to us every morning in school. A meal at lunch time was provided at very little cost.

These meals were high in protein, potatoes, and vegetables and sometimes dumplings. They were brought to school in huge metal bins.

Rationing was extremely complex, things were rationed at different times and in different ways, according to availability. Most Sundays we were kept up to date by the Radio telling us of any changes etc.

Rationing started in January 1940. The first items on ration were 4ozs Butter, 12ozs Sugar, and 4ozs Bacon per week? Each. The rest of the food would go on to ration when there became a shortage.

In July 1940 the allowances were approximately: Meat. 1shilling and 10 pence each (Sausages, liver, kidneys, tripe was not rationed but hard to get), Tea 2ozs each, butter,marg,cooking fats and cheese marg, 9p day each.
Sugar cut to 8ozs. No more bananas fresh or tined fruit, except oranges which were only for children.

In January 1945. We could have Whale meat, horse meat and Snoek (Fish).

Eventually the following became rationed Jam etc, cheese, and eggs.
Meat ration reduced to 1/6d. Milk, Dried Fruits, sweets, chocolate, rice, dried fruits, sweets, chocolate and Bread.

The last things to come of ration were:- Butter, cheese, marg and cooking fats.
Meat and Bacon in June 1954

Apparently the Food Minister quoted" Wartime Rations had helped the British to get healthier than they had ever been"

To enable people to have a little extra at Christmas

Mum had a sweet club not a money saving club but a coupons savings club.
When we got a sweet order she would take out the best of the items and save them up stairs till Christmas, the people who were in the club gave their coupons to save.

These were sent off to the Food Office with the rest of the coupons. They had to balance with the deliveries we had. By the time we got to Christmas it was difficult trying to sort out who had what. In the shop there was a large book which Mum kept all the details of how many coupons people had saved.

It always worked out well at the end, it was taking a chance on what would be delivered, as soon as they were put on sale they had gone within the hour.

Besides sweets we had cigarettes Black Cat, Woodbines,Players Weights, Players medium, Senior Service, and Dunhill again as with the sweets you did not know when you were going to get another delivery. Mum used to sell the cigarettes in 2s and 3s for people who could not really afford cigarettes.

Thinking about it now, it was not a good idea. It encouraged people to smoke who perhaps would have given up if they were not able to get them. While writing about cigarettes, I have remembered a prank Ann and I played on the Boys. I can not remember any of my school girl friends ever trying to blackmail me for sweets, but the boys did.

Ann's Dad worked on the Docks, he could get almost anything he wanted.
He rolled his own cigarettes, he was very good at it. Two of the boys had pestered me for some time, about getting them cigs.

Ann and I decided to roll them one each, using her Dads rolling machine, we waited till there was nobody in her house and went in.

My Mum used loose Typhoo Tea. I emptied the Tea Pot, and dried the tea leaves just leaving them a little damp.

We were in her house nearly all afternoon trying to roll them on the machine, we were just about to give up when her Dad came home. Of course he asked us what we were trying to do. He ended up rolling them for us they were very well done. We gave the boys one each, how we kept our faces straight, I do not know.

As they were trying to smoke them there were bits dropping out and they went blue with trying to draw on them.

A couple of weeks later they asked me what they were called. I said Pams make.
They said they were awful, laughing they asked what I meant by Pam's make.
These boys were only 10 or 11, I do not think they

had ever seen tobacco, never mind smoke it. When I told them about the tee leaves they busted out in laughter. It cured them they did not ask for ciggies again.

For quite some time the story went round School, and everybody joined in laughing.

On Brindle heath Road which was very long there were 2 Grocers, 1 Greengrocer, 2 Sweet Shops, 1 Butcher, 1 Gents Hairdresser, 1 Post Office, 1 Newspapers shop, 2 General Stores and 1 Pub.

Everything we needed was in these shops except of course the windows were always empty.

The goods never stayed in the shops any longer than a couple of hours. Before you could say" Jack Robinson" they had gone did not even have time to take them out of the boxes, never mind time to display them in the window.

To give some idea of the lay of the land, if standing with your back to the shop, on the right was a pub, then a one sided street, an unadopted road. This started Dornies Hills.

These Hills were used as a tip for coal coke etc. These hills stretched for about half a mile. Opposite the Hills were the Railway sidings. Directly opposite the shop was St Ann's School and church. In-between the school and the start of the Hills was a cobbled brew which led to Charles St.

I have happy memories of this street it was where we had the party for the end of the war.

Because all the shops were in our Road, I used to look in all the shop windows for a notice of when we could go for our rations usually the next day.

Sometimes Mum would let me go to get what we wanted, I should not say what was wanted, it should have been what you were given.

Sometimes if you were really unlucky you would get half a pound of dripping.
This is where the saying "dripping buttie came from - The North.

You would ask what was for tea; it could be a dripping buttie or a Jam buttie.
Every thing we had was made into the good old northern butties. Really it was just not the north that had everything on a butties, Everybody, North, South, East and West made butties of everything to fill up.

The girls decided to have a May Pole to get some money for the soldiers boxes and the evacuated children, we put on quite a good show regardless of the materials we had. The May Queen was chosen by how much they collected over a certain period of time.

We carried on after the war and each one was better than the one before.

We had a telegram informing us that Ted was lost in action. There a no words to explain how you felt when you received this kind of news. About two months later we received another telling us that Ted had returned to camp with his platoon after getting lost on manoeuvres.

What I am now going to tell you did not have a happy ending like Teds event.

Mum had a brother called Sid who had a son called Sid. Known as Ginger because of his red hair. Uncle Sid received a telegram telling him Ginger had been Killed, how was to follow. Ginger was a German Prisoners in Stalag 3, the prisoners wore various parts of uniforms, mainly German and Italian.

About 18 were marching from point one to point two. Two of OUR aircraft came over and because they were dressed in German uniforms they thought they were Germans. They did not leave the site till they had gunned down the entire group dead. Uncle could not get over this, and grieved for him till the day he died.

Attached to St Ann's school there was St Ann's

church. Like all churches a roll of remembrance was called every Sunday morning.

You could see in all the faces nothing but grief. When you were out you only had to look in the peoples eyes you could see nothing but despair.

Sunday school played a good role for the children, it was in the School Hall starting at 2pm. This was a haven for the children; we had a religious story, and then drew a picture of the story with crayons. School ended about 2 hours later.

I enjoyed Sunday school, in fact when I was about 13 I took a class, after the story I took packets of doilies and crayons they enjoyed colouring them and took the home for their mums to use on plates.

The boy's main recreation was collecting Shrapnel. They used to find out where had be bombed the previous night and go shrapnel searching. The object was to have a meeting for all the boys and do swaps for larger pieces.
While searching for shrapnel they would also collect wood - anything that would burn.

On Dornis hills the Coal Board used this place for tipping little bits of coal coke and dust. This coke came from industries with furnaces. When coal is burned all the gas is taken out of it. What is left is coke, the best of this was sold to coal merchants.

Who sold it to the public, any that was too small to sell was Tipped on these hills.

We were also sold anthracite again a Bi-product of coal and coke. Again if this was not good enough to sell it was tipped with the coal and coke.

One Sunday morning I was playing whip an top when 4 of the local lads came roaring down from the hills waving their hands in the air, very excited. They had found some red smooth stuff in strands like thick laces, little squares and other red bits. Nobody, not even our parents knew what this was, like the children they had never seen it before. It caused great interest and took quite a long time after to find out what it was.

When I first heard about Roswell (USA) and the material which was found that had not been seen before in 1947? I understand now how to find something and not know what it is.

Is very annoying and interesting at the same time? After all the excitement one of the parents found out what it was. It was just Plastic which some firm had dumped there.

Little did we know then what a big part Plastic would take? In our lives.

You would see people running to the hills with old prams - anything with wheels on and collect as much as they could, Coal; coke anything to take home to make a fire.

The boys also collected this and were always being told off about using it for a bonfire instead of leaving it for the people.

Every year we had a guy fawkes. He had straight black hair almost covering one of his eyes. A moustache and the boys had a name for him HIT.
He also had a girl friend called Eva. I wonder who this could be!!!!!.

On bonfire night we did not have fireworks at all, but sometimes somebody acquired black treacle and sugar. Then we had treacle toffee and baked potato some times it would only be a half a potato.

Something I could never understand was why the boys sent the girls home before they went home. I had to wait till after the war to find out.

Another prank of the boys was to annoy the Parkies. We had 3 Parks in our area; they would go with the intention of playing tricks on him.

Swimming in the nude in what we use to call the Cut. Tying string to letter box knockers, run round the corner and knock on the door by pulling the string, again to annoy people. Some of the Girls joined them from time to time (umumum) I wonder which girls?

They loved to annoy the girls especially when they were playing skipping ropes, we ended up with a mass of knots in the rope. It took ages to get them straight after they had finished with them.

There were usually 6 or 7 girls playing ropes, we took it in turns to bring the rope.

We would be playing Eva, Iva, over, when one of the girls Mums would arrive shouting have you taken the washing line out of the yard again? Of course the answer was yes.

Washing lines were hard to get, some of the lines the girls brought out had already been used for ages and ages and could not be replaced. It was easy to sneak in and pinch the line.

Other games were played by the girls.
Bobbers and Kibs. *The kibs were set out on the ground far apart. The Bobber was a hard rubber ball about as large as a grape. The Bobber was bounced on the ground. Before you caught the Bobber you had to pick up the Kibs with one hand. The person who has the most Kibs wins.*
Whip and Top. *The top is coloured by chalk. Wrap the whip round the top. The object was to spin the top with the whip, and keep it spinning by whipping it.*
Two Balls *was played with two balls on a smooth wall. Below are the key words to play with this game:*
Over. *Throw one ball over, not straight.*

Under. Throw one ball under leg.
Baker. Put one hand on hip.
Rounder. Throw one ball round back.
Dropsy. Let one ball drop on floor.
Upsie. Throw one ball up.
Slamsie. Slam one ball on floor aiming to hit the wall.
The idea is to sing or say the following, and play with out dropping the ball, following the key words:
One two three and OVER four five six and OVER seven and OVER
Catch the ball; carry on without stopping then next
One two three and UNDER four five six and UNDER seven and UNDER catch the ball (no stopping)
Carry on as above using the key words.
The winner is the one who gets the furthest.

We had another game -salt, mustard, vinegar, pepper. This was played on 4 steps. You could tell who played this by all the bruises and plasters on their knees and legs. We must have been mad.

The School opposite had 6 steps at the front door. The object of the game was to name the bottom step Salt, next one up mustard, the next one vinegar, the 4 up, pepper. One person at a time stood on salt, the caller shouted Vinegar, the one on the steps jumped from salt to Vinegar, then mustard, then pepper, or in any order. You had to jump from one step to the other without touching another step this had to be done quickly. When you were out you took the place of the caller. The winner was the caller who called the most.

In other words who got the most people out. The boys also played this game sometimes, we would all go to the Park collecting Conkers for the boys.

The radio played a big part in our lives - we had quite a selection of programs. Workers Playtime, Children's Hour with Larry the Lamb. Hit Mar, Dick Barton Special Agent, Old Mother Riley, and Toy Town. We had boxing fights with boxers such as Bruce Woodcock, Freddie Mills, Tommy Far, Lee Harvey and many more.

We used to have a bet on who would win. My penny always went on Bruce Woodcock. Poor Mum, Dad and Ede nearly always lost. Three pence winnings, I saved it for the next trip to The Cinema.

Peter Brough and Archie Andrews the ventriloquist were also on the Radio occasionally!!!!!!! I could never sort out which was Peter and which was Archie.

Not to forget the infamous "Lord HAW HAW" (William Joyce). He was a propagandist for the Germans. He broadcast from Nazi Germany with a sneering manner as he spoke. This is how he got the nick name Lord Haw Haw. He was born in New York USA in April 1906. He lived in Ireland then moved to London in 1921. 1932 he joined the Fascist Party under Oswald Mosley, and became leading speaker for The British Union of Fascists. In Aug 1939 just before

Time To Remember

the war he and his family moved to Germany just after he was tipped off that British intended to detain him, under Defence Regulations.
He became a naturalised German in 1940.

His radio announcements always started with. This is "Germany calling" "Germany calling" ", Germany calling. The content of his broadcasts were ment to demoralise the British Into surrendering, by saying such things as how many battles The Germans had won, and what he was going to do with us.
Joyce was arrested on the German-Denmark border. He was tried and executed on three counts of high treason.
1. Did aid and assist the enemies of the King by broadcasting to the Kings subjects propaganda on behalf of the Kings subjects
2. Did aid and comfort the Kings enemies by purporting to be a naturalised as a German citizen.
3. Broadcasting to the Kings subjecting them to propaganda on behalf of the Kings enemies.
It came to light that if treason is committed it must be against your own country. As he was born in America this caused a problem. This problem was resolved, he held a British Passport which was valid therefore he was classed as British.

Joyce was executed on 3rd January 1946 age 39 he was hung at Wandsworth Prison by Albert Pierrepoint. He went to his death unrepentant and defiant.

I must mention Vera Lynn,(Dame Vera) she was

given the OBE in 1969 and made a Dame by the Queen in 1975. She was given the name "The Forces Sweetheart" by the Troupes' who loved her. She had a concert Party and travelled to all overseas camps to entertain the troupes. She took with her celebrities of the time. She took them overseas to entertain the troupes'
The songs she sang became very popular.

One day when I was being a bigger pest than usual, Mum and Dad were listening to a report on the Radio. I kept annoying them and ended up crying.
They were trying to listen to what was being said. On the 7th Dec 1941, The Japanese bombed Pearl Harbour. I remember Mum saying this would bring America into the war. Which it did on the 8th Dec 1941 America declared war on Japan.

On 11th Dec 1941, Germany declared war on America. After this date we had a large build up of American Forces in the British Isles, training for the advance on Germany.

The first time I ever heard of TV was on the Radio. Very few people had TV; only the affluent could afford them. Our parents told us about TV how fantastic it sounded. We could not wait to get one. All TV programmes stopped broadcasting from 1939 to 1946.

Not long before the war ended we had a new customer

in the shop, his name was Albert he was a very nice man but sad at the same time. He was a Contentious Objector, he said he would be a driver, but would not kill.

He was accepted as a driver and sent to Germany. He drove in convoys taking supplies and ammunition to various depots. The drivers were told not to stop under circumstances for anything or any body.

He was horrified at the number of people he killed on the road. He was driving over men women and children who were trying to get on the moving vehicles.
He had a nervous breakdown, and was sent home. We now move on towards the end of the War.

The bombing of Pearl Harbour by the Japanese in Dec.41 had taken place, and Germany had declared war on USA in Dec 41. This war was indeed a world war affecting Poland, Canada, Denmark, Norway, Belgium, Holland all countries in Europe, and the Baltic States, Egypt, Athens, Greece, Russia. Brazil, Phillipines.North Africa, Burma and many more.
The BBC gave us the news that on the 6th Aug 1945 the USA bombed Hiroshima, and on the 9th Aug bombed Nagasaki, giving hope that this would end the war. Everybody cheered when this news came. Little did we know what kind of bombs had been used. We all cheered when this news came, little did we know what carnage and suffering these Atom Bombs caused.

Pamela Thompson

Was it worth it? - Some times I think yes and sometimes no.

To see the suffering on the Cinema, it was worse than anybody could have imagined.

Chapter Three
POSTWAR AND AFTERMATH

However on the 8th May 1945. VE day was declared, also VJ day was declared on 15th Aug 1945. There was elation all over, flags flying, bands playing, singing and dancing in the streets, everybody went to a victory party.

Ours was held on Charles St. Things that suddenly turned up at these parties were surprising. People must have been saving for this day. They produced sandwiches, cakes, biscuits, and all sorts of goodies, the children all received a present. I still have mine it is a little China pot with" made in Japan "on the bottom. Only about 4" high full of sweets, I still have the pot, but of course the sweets have been eaten.

 At this time everybody was elated that the war was over. It was not until we started going to the cinema and saw, The Pathay News Reels of our soldiers coming home in bandages, on sticks, all wounded trying to get off the ships which had brought them home. Their families on the dock side, who could not get to their husbands, brothers, sisters and friends of the ships quick enough.

The children meeting their Dads, some for the first time.

The most horrible had not yet been told to the world. The despicable Auschwitz, .Birkenau, Dachau, Belson (to name a few). When these concentration camps were liberated by our troupes, the Americans and Russians, they could not believe what they saw. We first heard over the Radio what had been found. It was bad enough to hear it, when it came on the news reel, it was heart breaking. How could any human being treat another in that way.

To me the answer was they are not human. I am sure this must have been one of the most horrible tradgedies in Human History.

As far as the children knew a war were just soldiers fighting soldiers - not genocide and cruelty to others. As far as I am concerned I could not believe what they were telling us, it came as a shock when I found out it was.
It was reported that Hitler and Eva Browne had committed suicide in his bunker in Berlin. Twenty one of the Leading Nazis were tried a convicted.
On 20/11/1945 the trial started at the Major War Criminal court in Nuremberg.
All twenty one pleaded not guilty.

There were also very many more trials, held at different Courts. They were put into various groups according to what roll they played in the atrocities.

Below are the sentences for the most notorious.
Boreman = Death.
He did not appear for the trial. In his Absence he was given the Death Sentence.

Goring = Death
He asked to be shot not hung. He thought that hanging was not acceptable for a man in his position. The Judges would not agree to this. He waited up to the night before his execution for them to change their minds, when they did not he committed suicide by taking Cyanide pills.

Hess = Life in prison
He served his sentence in Spandu Prison. He committed suicide in Spandau,
in 1987 at the age of 93.

Ribbentrop = Death
He was hung in 1946.

Spear = 20 years in prison
Which he served.

Goebbels = Death
He committed suicide before his trial. The trial took place without him, and he was given the Death penalty in his absence.

Eichmann = Death

He escaped to Argentina. He was ceased in 1960 and put on trial by Israel and hung 1962.

Himmler = Poisoned himself before his capture.

I suppose the trials were little consolation as punishment. Everybody wanted to know what had happened to the rest of the partakers, those who had worked in the camps etc.

There were so many trials, tried at different courts we did we did not really find out what the outcome was.

One of Hitler's passions was to produce a "Master Race" - People of Aryan decent with, blond hair, blue eyes, and pale skin. He professed that under his guidance, the world would be inhabited by Pure Aryans in 1000 years time.

He started his quest by bringing in a programme called. "Lebensborn" (Font of Life) which he called an Orphanage. Children were taken from their homes and kept in this orphanage till Aryan family were available. There were approximately 10.000 German and 9.000 Norwegian children taken for this reason. Those deemed not fit to be Aryans were taken to the camps.

Lebensborn"(Font of life) also housed women who were thought fit to bear Aryan children.

They were told to bear these children for the Fuhrer. These women had to produce Aryan children by Officers and men with Aryan features, as and when required. It has been estimated that about 7,000 children were born this way. What stories the Mothers, sons and daughters could tell. None of them knew who their Mothers and Fathers were or if they had brothers and sisters.

Some of these children along with adults, who were, Gypsies, Orphans, Mentally Ill, Disabled, Physically Handicapped, sets of Twins, and those who did not have Aryan features? - They were sent to "Mendlers" experimental hospital. For use in his experiments. His specialities were Identical and Conjoined Twins.

Sorry I can not go into this, its too upsetting.

I am just going to tell you about my "Stiff Neck"

I do not know how old I was when this happened, all I can remember is everybody having a good laugh at me.

I was suffering with a very painful neck. If I did not move my head, there was no pain. Moving it just a little, hurt like mad. I carried on for about a month without going to see the Doctor. When I did eventually go, he gave me a note for ointment, I went to the chemist, when I gave her the note she looked

puzzled and said I do not recognise this ointment and called out for help.
An assistant came out and looked at it and said, look in the deleted items book it may still be available.
They found it in the book; its name had been changed. I got home and could not wait to put some on my neck was killing me. I carried on for 2 weeks with it, it made no difference at all, Ede said she would get me another note, off she went and came back with 2 tubes.

After 4 or 5 weeks it did get a little better, Ede and I went back to the Doctors for another tube in case it came back.

The lady at the chemist was new, we had not seen her before. We gave her the note and I told her my neck was getting better. She disappeared round the back of the shop, came back and asked me did I say my neck was getting better? When I said yes she looked at Ede and I, and smiled, I am sorry she said, but you have not been using the correct ointment.
She let us look in the book that gave names of deleted items with the names of up to date equivalents. This is where the mix up happened. In those days we did not have the Health Service, the notes the Doctor were called Notes and any pills etc, had to be paid for. Mum had spent around 50d on the 3 notes for ointment, for my Stiff Neck, to find out that for 7 or 8 weeks I had been using ointment for "Piles".

The aftermath of the war was surprising to the adults,

and particularly the children. Everybody expected the rationing to stop as soon as the War finished. This did not happen in fact rationing was to get worse before it got better. Nobody even considered that rationing would go on till 52-53. The last thing to go on ration was Bread in July 1946. During the war up to 1946 the bread we had was called "The National Loaf" it was a Wholemeal loaf, far more Wheat was used which meant less wastage, but more time in the toilet.

The first item to come off ration was Bread in 1948. The last thing to come of ration was Meat and Bacon in June 1954. Many of our food requirements such as fruit, sugar, and many kinds of raw materials used to manufacture our food had to be imported. This meant that we had to wait for foods coming in from overseas.

The first year after the war the Rations were fewer than ever. As children we had not seen things like Bananas, Grapes and many other Fruits. I remember my first banana, not the actual banana, the skin. My friend brought one to school, we could not wait till playtime just to look at it.

When the teacher found that Joan had one, she was just as interested as we were, she gave us a lesson on where they came from and how they were grown.

Miss Burton asked Joan if she thought it was a good idea to cut it up and give a little each to the class.

Talking about a Loaf and Five Fishes, how about A Banana and 40 children? The actual banana was cut up into the smallest of pieces. The skin was also cut small. If you scraped your teeth on the skin you got the flavour of the Banana.

I remember we received our first food parcel about 2 months after the war we think it came from Australia.

I had my first bacon from out of a tin it was very nice. There was tined fruit, tins of luncheon meat, tined salmon, biscuits, and a tin of baked beans, in all these things the only thing I had eaten were baked beans, and a few biscuits.

During the war there were food parcels for families who had Dads away in the forces. These were distributed by The Salvation Army. They carried on for some time after the war. Where these parcels came from was not known, everybody who received them was delighted.

There were plenty of sketches in newspapers regarding the food shortages. One very popular one was Mr. Chad. It was a man looking over a wall, his finger tips were just showing on the top of the wall, also his nose was resting on the wall. His head was bald and he had a question mark over it. Under the wall depending what foods were not available. It would have written underneath. What no BACON

Time To Remember

or what ever was short. "What no Bread" (or any other item.)

Now we were able to order more or less what was available. Mum started a coupons and monies saving club again for Xmas. They ordered what was available. This only carried on for about three years, the volume of sweets we had filled a bedroom, and all the downstairs cupboards.

There were so many orders we had to ask people would they please come in and collect their parcel, when we told them there order was ready. We had nowhere to keep them when they were made up.

Eventually you could order from the supplier what you required, in hope you would get it.

The customers were delighted at Christmas Time. After all the years unable to buy chocolate, it was great to see their children's faces.

In the cellar we had a half barrel, with the top sawn off, it had inside a cylindrical contraption with 2 blades one at each side and a handle you turned.

This was in the cellar when my mum bought the shop from my Aunty it was a hand ice cream maker, what a job. It took ages to make one batch of Ice Cream. Mum use to order the Ice from Smithfield Market in Manchester.
The following had to be done quickly as possible.

Mum made the Ice cream mixture with milk, eggs and sugar. All these ingredients were boiled together then left to go cold. What follows next was my Dads Job he packed the Ice tightly round the barrel and then the cold the mixture into the cylinder. Then the hard bit, for about 3 hrs he turned the handle of the Churner in the Barrel and kept filling up the Ice as it melted. Eventually the Ice Cream was ready, my job was to clean the churner blades, it was a great job, spooning all the Ice cream off (um um) This was good old-fashioned ice cream yellow not white like it is today.

The shop soon became known as Smithies Ice Cream Shop. The people came from all over for Ice Cream. I did have the recipe, but it has got lost.

Only 1 batch of ice cream could be made at any one time and the demand was heavy. Dad carried on with this contraption for about one year. He was really fed up with it.

Out of the blue he started knocking 7 bells out of the side counter. Mum was going mad with him; he would not tell her what he was doing. This went on for 3 days, on the 4th day a lorry pulled up outside the door. The driver shouted where do you want this to go Mrs? To Mums amazement it was an electric ice cream maker. All mod cons now.

It looked like a twin tub washing machine but larger it was great it only took quarter of a hour to make from when the mixture was ready. Instead of 3hours by hand, this is what he was making room for, and wanted it to be a surprise for Mum. It saved a lot of work for Dad.

On the right of the machine there was the churner and on the left a storage compartment.

My dad again had an idea he kept bringing home blocks of wood, he would sit there for hours cutting up little sticks when Mum asked what he was doing he just grinded and carried on. One day he arrived home with about 6 dozen egg cups. And orange cordial yes he was going to make ice lollies. He arranged one layer of egg cups round the bottom of the storage container then he balanced another layer on the first layer and carried on this way till they were about 5 layers high. Then he dropped in the sticks he made. I was always in trouble my latest thing was slamming the counter door next to the ice cream machine, and the cups would all fall except for the bottom tier, this always happened when he had just put the cordial in and nowhere near frozen.

First the lollies were half a penny each, then 1p. Then 2p Dad could not make them quick enough, people came for miles for Ice Cream and lollies.
When the raspberry and strawberry sauces came out dad put a table and bench in the shop and made ice cream with either strawberry or raspberry on, something that younger people had not had.

The cellar was also used as a bath room. The old tin Lizzy was filled by ladle with hot water from the Old-fashioned boiler which was built with a bricks. There was a door directly under the boiler. It was fired by coal or coke.

When hot enough Ede and I would ladle out the water and share the Tin Lizzy.
One at each end, this was to save 2 lots of water. It was always warm in the cellar when the fire had been lit.

There was an Old Fashioned Mandel in the cellar. A Mandel is a hand operated machine with two rollers when the handle was turned the washing went between these two rollers and squeezed out the water.

The coal was tipped from the window outside down into the cellar.

All the washing was done in the cellar.

Dad came home from work one day, he had won a Chicken at work, in a raffle.
When he was given his prize he was shocked, it was a Chicken but it was alive. The man at Work who provided the Chicken for the Raffle.
Had a Chicken Coup in one of his bedrooms. He did this because when it was in the Garden he had no way to stop the theft of his Chickens, which provided

him a small income. He told Dad to try strangling it first if this did not work chop off its head.

He took it down the cellar, after a few minutes there was a noise. Dad was shouting and a skirmish took place. He came flying up from the cellar as white as a sheet. He could not strangle it, so he chopped off its head. The shouting was the fact that the chicken ran round the cellar and up two steps with no head on. The man who told him to chop it off did not tell him that, the nerves in its neck stayed alive for a few seconds when its head was chopped off.

The year that the above happened came to be known as the Year of the Chicken and the Turkey, because of the following.
Mum was friendly with the greengrocer whose shop was round the corner over a croft.
At Christmas we were all expecting our ration of a half turkey. On Christmas Eve Mum went to collect our half Turkey. It was thick with fog, we were all wondering what had happened to her she was away ages. At last she came back very upset, she was clinging to a dirty thin Half Turkey.

She had dropped it on the croft and could not find it. The fog was very thick, after searching and searching she found it. She could feel that she had trodden on something. Looked down and it was the turkey, it had fallen into a mass of wet mud. No way was this turkey going to be thrown out it was

scrubbed and washed till it was like new. We all enjoyed our Christmas lunch.
This was the first time I had Turkey.

When you went to collect your rations from various shops you were lucky if you got what you wanted. Going to the butchers for your meat ration was very dodgy. All the shop keepers put a notice in their windows informing us when the next order was due. This caused everybody to make sure they got their ration. From memory it was something like 1 chop per week each, Quarter pound Meat or Sausages.

Everywhere you went there was a long queue. You would stand at the end and watch the customers get served and think good only four or five person in front of me. You would be very lucky if they had anything left when it came your turn.

On one occasion when I went to the butchers. After being in the queue only a short time there was a man being punched about the face by a lady. She said he had pushed in, his nose was pouring in blood. The butcher closed the shop, till the following day.

Actually I was quite please this had happened. He was the man who used foul language to my friend and I, when we were collecting for the War Effort.

The first May after the war we decided to do May Poles again. Materials were still short but we managed with what we could get. This time the

money we collected all went to the children who had been evacuated? We decided to make Pompom Hats for the Boys and Girls. We were able to buy a very poor quality of wool, very coarse a bit like string in different colours. The hats were knitted by our mums, and the girls made the pompoms for the Hats. This was done by using two milk bottle tops, in those days, they were made of cardboard. The two tops were put together. Round with a hole in the centre, the wool was pushed through the hole in the middle and then continue putting
The wool through the hole till you could not get any more in. Push scissors between the two bottle tops and cut round the edge. While the tops were still together put 3 strands of wool together, to make it stronger put this in-between the two tops and pull hard to secured the middle then pull the tops apart. Roll in your hands and fluff up giving you a pompom. These were then stitched onto the hats, then given to the collector for despatch to the Evacuees.

These dispatch depot is where everything that was made went to be dispatched. Nearly all the money from the May Pole was spent on the children.

The making of the May Pole was good fun. The stale from a yard brush or mop was decorated with coloured paper which we acquired from the local Printers. Some times there would be crape paper in the parcel. Six long strings were attached to the top of the pole one for each of the girls.

Each had a skirt and hat made from paper. They would take a string each.
In two lots of three they skip round, each three plaiting a string, ending up with 2 Plaits.

While they were doing this we would all sing. "We come to great you hear today and we hope you will not turn us away on a May Pole Day"

The May queens dress was always white, she held a Red Cross tin.

For the collection to be made, where it came from we did not know. This was done outside peoples homes they put something in the tin. The most lucrative was the pub. Publican would say come in but be as quick as possible before the Police come in. We would sing and dance as quickly as possible, so we could get out as quick as possible in case the police came in.

The May Poles carried on for a long time after the war. In the North it was a challenge to see who could make the best May Pole. They became very elaborate and pounds were spent on them.

Back to School now for the Christmas Parties. These took place on the last day at School before Christmas. Each child took something towards the party, the goodies which were brought in, would all be set out on the desks which had been pushed together in the morning?

These parties should have been called Jelly and Jam buttie parties. You would never be sure what goodies would be brought in. There were approximately 40 in the class. You could guarantee there would be at least 35 jellies, a few Potted meat Butties, home made cake and biscuits. Again depending what ingredients could be found. The bottle of milk which was provided by the Council in the mornings, was saved for the afternoon. There was never enough cake and biscuits to go round. Sometimes we had half a cake or biscuit each

After we would play charades and find the parcel. They were happy times a couple of hours away from home. The families had constant worries, not only where the next Meal was coming from. Or having enough monies.

Even though the War was over, everybody who had a family member,
Friends or anybody who had been in the War and was not home lived in fear of the telegraph boy coming on his bike.

Everybody who saw him would be afraid they were going to get either to get Killed in Action or Lost in action just like we did when the War was on. Even the children got upset when they saw him around on his bike.

Attached to St Ann's School was St Ann's Church.

Like all the churches a roll of remembrance was read every Sunday morning. You could see all these people with grief all over their faces. When you were out you only had to look at some of the grief stricken faces. And you knew perhaps they had received a telegram.

Ede was not needed for munitions work now the War was over. She was able to help Mum who by this time, was extremely bad on her legs.

The company Ward & Goldstones brought out peace work, which was done at home?

Nearly everybody in the area did this work. It was one of the ways to earn monies.

You could tell who did this work by their sore thumbs and first fingers on both hands.

The task was to put tiny screws into the nuts, to hold the wires firm.
Which were then used in electric plugs, this will give you some idea how small the screws were. These nuts, screws and tiny screwdriver were brought to your home by the thousands. The most boring job you can not imagine.
Ede used to sing after a while it was so boring, she always wondered why we sat there with cotton wool in our ears.

The children of the families who did this work,

Time To Remember

thought at first it was a game, till they got fed up with them and would disappear when they were brought out.
I am not sure I think it was about 20d for a box 1000. The work had a nick name "The slaves Job".

Because all the families only had one gas light in the house they used to do the screws out side on the step weather permitting.

Round the corner from the shop there was a family in a 2up and 2down house with 8 children. Their father did not work (perhaps he did not have time) he did the screws in his spare time. It was like a day out to them all sat on the step doing screws. All accept one of the daughters. She would not do any, she used to come home and say, very proudly that she was not doing screws.
She was going out.

One day she came in the shop and introduced us to Cloe. Cloe was absolutely beautiful, black curly hair, lovely features, especially her eyes, petite and a lovely smile. Her Dad could not understand how Cloe came to be black. I believe his wife had to explain how.

I will say no more about this except that near to where we lived we had a USA Airforce Base at Burtonwood. Manchester and the surrounding towns had thousands of airmen who came in for entertainment.

It was about this time when Ede took on the job of Mum. She took me everywhere with her even though I was a pest. I remember very clearly her taking me to the dentist to have one tooth out. When we got there the dentist said she needs 7 out. Ede reluctantly said ok, when I came round from the Gas she was crying. All the way home she did not know what Mum would say when she saw me without 7 teeth. When Ede saw me eating all my tea she knew I was OK.

Big changes were about to take place in the shop and house. The rules lay down by the Ministry of Health called for any premises used to manufacture food, had to have certain things, such as hot and cold water, water boiler, a sink and a room for this purpose only.

Mum used to make the Ice Cream in the kitchen which only had cold water, a small round gas ring to boil the Ice Cream on... This called for Dad to get rid of his birds from the shed.

He gave the Birds and Breading Cages to Pet Shops. We then had the shed free; a sink was put in with hot and cold water, and a work bench.

The living room fireplace was taken out and a back boiler installed in the new one.

To Edes and my delight we had the small back

bedroom made into a bathroom, this meant that we could say good by to the Tin Lizzy and Ladle.

The bath took one wall up with a sink next to it, no toilet, that was still in the yard.

Next to the fireplace we had put the back boiler in down stairs, we had a cupboard which was a good airing cupboard. It was always nice and worm, it was a big help to Mum she used it to raise the bread she had made.

Again I found my self in trouble I loved the bread mixture raw. When it was in the cupboard I would sneak in and pinch a bit, if you disturbed the mixture while it was raising it would not rise again in the place where it had been disturbed. I loved it, but Mum went mad with mad with me, but it was worth it.

We had two Bakers in the area, they were encouraged to have yeast and flour for sale by the Government hoping that it would encourage people to make their own.

My job was to go a get Yeast and flour. Because I always gave him a big grin he would give me yeast to eat on my way home.

You could only buy unsliced loaves in the shop. Our Baker made a batch of rolls and balm cakes nearly every day to give us all a treat. If you were early enough after school you could get Rolls and Balm Cakes from the Baker, depending on what he had left.

The smell of newly made bread was good, with butter on it. It went down a treat. I can make a meal of Bread and Butter and a cup of tea.

We had not had the bathroom very long, when I had a mishap.

I bet that not many people have done what I did. I belonged to the Church Youth Club, on one occasion we went on a hike to Glossop. The weather was awful rain making every where muddy and wet. Everybody had mud all over their hair, on our legs all over.

When I got home I had mud everywhere and very tired. Mum said put some Soda in the bath it will help the aches and pains. I went down to the cellar to get the soda to put in my Bath. After a while I noticed that the water was going slimy. I thought it was all the mud I had on me, so I took no notice. When I got out of the bath my skin felt smooth, shiny and stiff. When I got down I asked my Mum to feel my skin, did you put the Soda in she said, yes was the answer.

Ede went up to the bathroom and came down laughing, in her hand she had a box and ask me was that what I had put in the bath? She gave mum the box then Mum started to laugh.

I had not put soda in, it was "Starch" I did not live it down for ages.

Whit Week Walks, The Church of England walked on Good Friday.
Catholics on Easter Monday. All churches put on a procession which started at the Church and ended in Leaf Square about a mile away. A service was held when everybody arrived, then we made our way back to church where we had a party. All the girls were dressed all in white, dress, shoes and socks, and vale, which was held in placed by a head dress of small white flowers.
The boys wore dark trousers and white shirt. Mums saved up nearly all year to buy these clothes. The children formed little groups the boys carrying the banners, and large centre pieces which had six ribbons.

The girls took a ribbon each and walked with the centre piece. They looked forward to getting, new cloths etc. Many children could not afford the expense, but they were still allowed to join the walk.

One year there was a heat wave on the day of the walks, shoes, socks, fingers were full of "pitch" today tarmac is used. The roads were covered with "pitch," when it was hot bubbles formed, all the children use to love popping them with their feet and fingers. There must have been a lot of shoes discarded that day.

Every child had new clothes for Easter Sunday, even those who could not have new clothes for the walks. Mums saved up for these cloths weekly with the local Drapers. The shop was in most cases a normal house. They turned the front room into the shop and displayed the clothes in the small front window. You got everything you wanted, underwear etc... After Easter Sunday everything could only be used for Best, we had to wait till the next Easter Sunday before we could have any more, and then the new ones became your best. You always had a set of best and a set to wear.
You would go with your Mum to chose what you wanted, they would be put away by the Draper till a few days before they were needed.

Nearly all the coats had hats which we did not like at all, but we had to wear them. I do not know how my hats were found thrown over in gardens or stuffed under a hedge in the Park. The white dresses and veils were kept for our confirmation day.

Once again we started with bonfires. This time we had fireworks, sparklers, treacle toffee, toffee apples. Not a lot, we were pleased with what we had.

The second year they got more plentiful. Every week starting a few weeks before bonfire night, we took

Time To Remember

our spends to Clarks, he saved them each week for our fireworks. I sat on my bed counting them and putting them in order. Waiting for Bonfire night was like waiting for Christmas.

However Bonfire Night came after all the waiting. I am sure it is hard to understand why there was so much excitement. It was the first time we had these events. These things were new to us all. Even to go collecting wood for the Bonfire was an event. There was not shortage of things to burn, people were getting rid of their old furniture.

Once again the Guy forks looked like a man we and people all over the World hated him. We all stood round the Bonfire with fireworks, treacle toffee, sparklers and parkin.

Surprisingly I can only remember one time when anybody was hurt with a firework.

Bonfire night was when everybody got rid of things they did not want. One of the Dads had a set of drawers to burn, somebody put a banger in one of the drawers, when he was stood near the fire burning one draw at a time, the draw with the banger in, exploded, the man ended up with face burns.

One Bonfire Night, I was to find out why the boys always sent the girl's home, before they went home. I sneaked out and hid behind a wall. All the boys were stood in a circle round the Bonfire facing inwards and the fire was going out quite quickly. They were all sighing and had a look of relief on their faces. (I think I guessed correct, what do you think?)

For the first time we felt what it was like to live next door to a Pub. The beer was delivered by 4 Shire Horses pulling a lorry. The lorry stopped in front of the Pub. The horses were directly in front of the shop, they had to because the beer barrels had to be rolled down through a window leading to the cellar.
The horses made an awful mess out side the shop. They left a river running down the Road. The horses did what the boys did on bonfire night. They also left another bodily function. This was very soon moved. There were two brothers who had an allotment on the sidings, they used to watch for any horses and run round with a big shovel and hand cart and collected it, to use on their allotment as a fertilizer. This became quite a good business they sold it to the other allotment owners.

This was not the only problem we had with the Pub, the constant home coming parties for the soldiers in the Pub. They got a bit tiresome at times.
When they left the pub they carried on out side, leaving behind them the contents of their stomach. In those Day's closing time was 10.30pm.
We did not get to sleep till well after midnight.

Many of the soldiers seem to take a long time to get home. After the war people became very anxious

Time To Remember

about this and could not understand why it was taking so long for some people and not others. It did take a long time, it was nearly a year before Ted came home. Harry came home before him. Ede was pleased at this, he lived in Romford Essex. He took Ede to meet his family and they made plans to get married.

Ted eventually came home, what a day, about two weeks before he came home we had telegram from him to say he was back in the UK and would be home as soon a possible. Before he could come home he had to have medical treatment. Within 2 weeks we had a phone call from him saying he would be home the following day after 2pm. Nobody moved out of the house after 1pm that day. Mum and Dad were teetotal they would not have drink in the house. But for this day Dad relented and acquired bottles of beer. Teds home coming called for a drink. This was the only time I ever saw Dad have a drink.

We planned to close the shop when he got home. The time went so slowly, we thought he would never get home. 2pm 3pm 4pm time went on. Mum, Dad, and Ede, had not seen him for nearly 6years. I did not know him at all.
Ede was reminiscing about the games they played as children. Dad about the times he took him playing Tennis. At about 8-45 the door bell rang, there was a dash to the door. Mum was crying and Dad was not far of, Dad got to the door first, Mum and Ede were dying to get to him. I stood at the door between the

living room and Shop. To me he was a complete stranger.

I had visions of him being tall and well built like Dad. When I first saw him at the door, I was surprised to see him. He was not tall and well built he was about 5ft 6"and very thin. Dad and I were tall, Mam, Ede, and Ted small.
Never the less he was home safe. During the war he wrote to my future sister in law. Within a few months they were married. I then had a Mum, Sister, and sister-in-law all called Edith. For the short time he lived with us. I did not really know him, it was only when he had children I got to know him and visited him quite a lot. It was about this time when Harry got a V8 Pilot Shooting Brake. It was very big it held 3 on the front and three on the back seats.
Plus room for 2 small Arm Chairs in the boot space.

Ted mentioned he would like to see Maud at Wales.

To our amazement Dad said he would come. This was in the only time he wanted to go out, all he wanted was work and his home.

As usually when we went out, Mum made dinner plate Size Apple Pie and Whimbery Pie. (Think that's how To spell Whimbery)

Mum, Dad, Harry, Ede, Ted and Teds Edith and I piled into the car, after putting in the food, a small

Table, then the 2 Arm Chairs. It was a very hot day, and we went of in good spirits. About half way we broke down, Harry walked back to a garage which we had just passed, for a part for the car..
While he was gone we got the table, food and the arm chairs out and put them on the grass and have a drink.

As people went by they gave us a smile and a wave. It must have looked Granny Clampits and Muldoon's Picnic rolled into one. Mum said to me put the whimbery Pie back in the car. Which I did.

About one and a half hours later the car was fixed. Dad was wearing a very light grey pair of trousers. As we were all getting back in the car, Dad let out a big yell. He got out of the car and showed us his BUM. Gosh I was in trouble again; he had sat on the Whimbery Pie. Whimbery is a purple fruit, when made into a Pie it is very juicy. Mum gave me one of her looks. I did not mean put it on a seat, I meant in the back, she said. I had another black mark in my book.

Dad really surprised us all that day. When we got to Wales, Mum wanted to go and get him a pair of trousers, which he refused. Mum said she was not going to Mauds, with his trousers like that, he shook his head and said he would be ok. Mum really went to town on him, and when she called him Edwin we knew she meant it. Off she went and came back with trousers for him, which she hit him on the head with? Ede and I were giggling in the back, she gave us another look, she was mad at us. Mum was only 5ft 4inches tall and slim. When she got mad, nobody stood a chance.

Ted had 4 children Ted, Allan, Lynn and Carol in that order.

Do you remember me telling you about knocking the Ice Lollies over.

With in a couple of days Ted did the same thing. Just one difference I used to get told off. Ted did not they just grinned at him (Sulk, Sulk)

In 1948 Mum bought the local Fish and Chip Shop from Mrs Herring (good name for a Fish and Chip Shop owner). This shop was for Ede to manage, which she did for Quite a few Years. Ede also married in this year; she was married at St Ann's Church. I was a bridesmaid I thought I was the bee's knees in my long blue dress with pink circles on. My mum made it for me.

Not all Harrys family were able to come from Essex, just his Mother and one sister came to the wedding. Harry became manager of the local Dairy, he had not been there long when Ted joined him.

Ede and Harry bought a house further up Brindle-heath Road. It was not very long before Andrea came a long. I was an Aunty at 10years old. Over the years Andrea and I became very close, we were like sisters.

Mums health was not good Harry and Ede took me everywhere they went. The only time Ede really shouted at me was when we were on holiday in Wales. I had been paddling at the sea edge with Andrea, I let go of her hand and she went under. I reached out and grabbed her by the hair removing a hand full hair. Ede went absolutely mad at me. I made sure Andrea did not let go of my hand again.

There were a couple of things Ede went on to me about, She took over from Mum. They both used to say "You have not got your vest and Liberty bodice on", then pulled up my top and gave my midriff a good smacking. Ede was the worst she really gave me a good smack, this has gone on to this day.

Quite often in fun she will say where is your vest and liberty bodice, but she does smack me now. I think we all know what a vest is, but not sure about the Liberty Bodice. During the war many items of clothing, bedding, towels etc, were especially made for hard wear and warmth. Every thing made had a utility mark on which would not wash off. A Liberty Bodice was one of these things. It had no sleeves, a round neck, the material had a backing on for warmth. There were 4 buttons attached to the bottom, 2 on each side.
These were to button your suspenders on. They had no shape to them at all.

The suspenders were purchased in fours, they were made of rubber, they were taken off and put on when needed.

I can not find words (without being rude) to tell you what the knickers were like, so I will leave that one.

1952 and 1953, turned out to be very eventful, I left school at 15. Sweets came of ration in 1952 and Ede had David.

In 1952 the Rationing finished, sweets being the last thing. Mum had saved all the sweets she could which had been delivered by the supplier. The intention of saving them for when they came off Ration. The big day arrived it was a Sunday. The day before we spent arranging all the sweets in the window. It was good to see the window so full and set out nicely. It really looked like Aladdin's Cave. We had to keep the blind down because everybody seemed to watch us to see what we were doing. They were making up minds up what they were going to buy the next day.

Apart from this not being fair to the other customers. It was distracting for us so we put the blind down. The last thing we did was to put a notice in the window saying we would be open at 10am next morning.

It was nearly 1am before we got to bed very tired.

Mum and I shared the front bed room. At about 4am we were woken by laughing and giggling. I looked out side and found people were queuing - waiting for the shop to open.

We all got up and opened the shop at 10am. To our amazement there was not a sweet or chocolate left in the shop by 11am. In one hour it was all gone after spending months collecting it, then hours setting up the window. Every shop experienced the same sold out in no time.

After this it was just like when the rationing was on. We had to wait in some cases a month before we could get any more.

In 1953 Mum decided to sell the sweet shop as her legs got so bad she could hardly walk. Ede took over the Fish and Chip Shop. She bought the house next door but one to EDE on Brindleheath Road.

The first year I did not get a job, I stayed to help Mum till she sold the shop.
I worked for a Bureau where I could have time off if Mum needed me.
I had quite a few jobs sometimes I stayed 1 week only at some others it could be a year. I also had an evening job, I loved going to the cinema. I thought how about getting a job at the local cinema. I ended up selling ices. In those days an Ice Cream girl's job was to load the tray. Put the strap over your head and off you went backwards down the isles.

Not forgetting your torch. We walked backwards with the torch shining on the Ice Cream, tempting the public to buy. One night a new group of boys came in and they thought they would have a bit of fun. One of them sat down on the floor of the isle I was coming down. I went over him head first and landed on the arm of a seat. The manager came out looked at me and off we went to the hospital. I had 3 stitches in my head. After that we walked down the isle and stood at the bottom and the public came to us.

I can not remember what his title was, but this manager had something to do with all the cinemas. He reported my accident and suggested the Ice Cream.
Girls did not walk backwards. I was not long after that Ice Cream Girls did not walk backwards at any cinema.

Now that rationing had finished, we all felt free to have what we wanted. Not that it was always in the shop but you could order it. Everybody was in some form of savings club.

Notable Events 1945
Controversial Bombing of Dresden.
Hitler took his own life.
Mussolini Executed in Italy.
Germany surrenders to the Allies.
Nuremberg Trials start.
World counts the cost of war

55 million dead and scars of man`s
Capacity for evil.

Music
We`ll Gather Lilacs in the spring.

Films
Brief Encounter.
The bell`s of St Marys

Notable Dates 1946
Top Nazis executed at Nuremberg.
India rejects British plans for Independence.
Britain returned to war-time Rations.

Sport
The Derby back at Epsom after 6 years.
FA Cup Derby County beat Charlton Athletic 4-1

Notable Events 1947
Fifteen hundred coalmines are nationalised
By the Labour Government.
Coldest winter since 1881. 20ft snowdrifts.
President Truman's Communist "Witch Hunt".
Sport
Charlton Athletic beat Burnley 1-0 in FA Cup.
There was worry for some of the families their loved ones had not teturned home some decided to stay abroad.
Many just disappeared of the face of the earth.

Can you imagine how the families and friends felt not knowing?
What had happened to them?
They had not received a lost in Action or died in Action telegram.
Vast searches were made by the families, they first got in touch with the War Office, they could only tell them that discharge papers had been issued to them, and that was it.

The families gave all the information they had to such organisations as The Red Cross and a few more agencies.

A few of the soldiers were found, and contacted. They had a choice to stay or return home. I do not know how many were eventually contacted. It must be terrible to loose somebody and never know what has happened to them.

Toni a customer, who came in the shop, told us about the day they received the news that the War was over. When they returned from exercise most of the Soldiers were having a meal, the Quartermaster came in and gave them the official news that the War was over. Toni remembered a young soldier who threw his hat in the air and danced around singing and shouting with glee, nobody could stop him. The Quartermaster told him to shut up and clear out. (We had a feeling it was Toni).

When it dawned on them many cried, they realised

they had survived. That evening they were all very quiet and subdued, thinking of their comrades who they had lost. With in a matter of days the elation they felt turned into worry, wondering what the future held for them. Missing the camaraderie they had.
Concern about rebuilding family life.

Notable Events 1948 and 1949
Mahatma Gandhi is assassinated.   1948
Baby boom 1948.
The National Health Service promises `Cradle to grave `care. 1948
NATO is formed. 1949
The Soviet Union becomes a nuclear power.   1949

Films
Hamlet.   1948
Oliver Twist.   1948
The Third Man   1949

Sport
At the London Olympics the Americans dominate the
Track with 38 Gold medals.   1948
Wolves beat Leicester City 3-1   1949

The main object was getting enough food for the family. Food was harder to get than in the War years.

Soldiers and evacuated children were coming home. Giving more mouths to feed.

It was a nightmare going shopping, queues were down the Road and
Round corners, far worse than the war years.

You would queue for as long as two hours. As you got near to the front of the queue, they would be sold out. Ede and I queued for 2hours for meat, flour, and anything that made a meal. We came back with a packet of Dried Egg.
Eggs were really the only thing we did not need. Dad had a friend at work that had a Chicken Coup, he supplied Mum with eggs to make the Ice Cream, it took 10 to make one batch.

The Food Office had adverts all over, trying to encourage people to make their own meals. They supplied dried milk, dried eggs, flour, yeast, lard, and many other items to the grocers who would get it to the public. Recipes for nutritious and cheap meals, were on the Radio and News Papers of the Day.
Recipe for Rabbit Pie with a crust, this was a good one. The country side had provided us with Rabbits during the War. It's a good job they are prolific breeders to keep us going. A Rabbit and Skirt meat makes a nice Rabbit Pie, with crust. Save the thick chunky legs when it had gone cold, it makes a nice buttie.

Hot Pot was another I am sure that most people have had Hot Pot. White Tripe and Cowheel Stew, Pigs Trotters, Brains, Sheep's Heads, Black Tripe, Bacon Ribs and Cabbage when available.

The only things I liked of the above and still have is Honeycomb or Seam Tripe (not cooked and out of the fridge) on a warm day it can be very refreshing. With salt and vinegar and a nice home grown tomato,Cabbage and Bacon Ribs.

With having a coal fire I used to enjoy sticking a good thick slice of Bread on the long toasting fork, you needed a long one, making it on an open fire it gets very hot, when done put butter on it. Make a nice cup of tea, coffee, coco or oxo. and sit near the fire on a cold night, and watch TV. I can make a meal of these thick chunks of toast, the problem was the flies were attracted to the butter and jam. Mum always had several old style Sticky Fly Catchers hung up either on the light or from the ceiling. Today it's good you just give a spray from the can and bingo they are dead.

We returned to war time rations, there was a fear there would be a World Wide famine.

In 1946 the ship Exodus landed with Jewish illegal immigrants. Sailing from France with approx 4,500 immigrants including approx 700 children. Other ships also carried illegal immigrants which had sailed from other ports.

The British decided to stop this by sending the ships back to where they came from. The Exodus was the first ship this applied to. When the "Exodus" reached the coast of Palestine. The British destroyers rammed the ship and boarded it. It was towed to Haifa. The immigrants were put on ships and sent back to France. When they arrived in France they would not get off the ship.
The French government refused to take them off. They spent 25 days on board during a heat wave, despite the lack of food and sanitary conditions.
The British decided to take them back to Germany. The Exodus sailed for Hamburg. Journalists who covered the story told the world of the heartlessness and cruelty of the British. The British changed there mind, they were not sent back to Germany. They were transported to detention camps in Cyprus.

The majority of the passengers on the Exodus settled in Israel, some had to wait till the State of Israel was announced.

The United Nations had its inaugural in Westminster. King George X1 and our priminister attended with representatives from 50 nations.
In 1947 Jewish refugees were turned away from Britain, as tens of thousands were seeking new homes.

Time To Remember

In 1948 the new state of Israel opened its doors to all Jewish immigrants.

It is so sad that nearly 70 years later, the situation between The Arabs and the Jewish have not been resolved. "Do you think it will ever?"

Some of the men tried to supplement their income by having an allotment or Pig Club. The allotments were on the railway sidings, the soil was not good at all, stones and clay. None of them were very successful. The Pig Clubs were very lucrative; they consisted of 8-12 men. They saved any waste to be collected for the pigs. They took out any waste that could be cured by any Butcher. It would be sold; any that could not be cured was sold as pig swill. Things like tongues, heads, inners, giblets any offal. this boosted the rations for some time.

Mum used to get an Ox Tongue very nice. As a matter of fact when I can get one I cook it at Christmas. They are hard to buy now, they are all used for commercial purposes. For those who buy Ox Tongue why not cook your own.
When the Tongue is taken out of the Ox and trimmed. It is soaked in Brine overnight (your butcher will do this for you, it must be soaked.) Do not put salt in the pan, boil it until the skin is coming off, take it out of the pan and skin it, if you have boiled it long enough the skin will come off easy. Put it in a basin or container that it fits in quite snug. Cover container with some form of lid and place a heavy

weight on it this will press it, when cold tip out. You will find it is the best Tongue you have every tasted. (Um a nice butty.)

As for the other things Brains etc no thanks.

The Black Market flourished again after the war; really it did not help those who did not have much money, Black Marketers purchased goods from the Shops in great numbers, and charged them at a profit. This made shortages worse, not leaving any goods for the people to buy. This was referred to as "under the counter"

Mr Chad was still peeping over a wall; he became more popular than he was before. Not only did he appear in newspapers etc, the populace used his "What no Sugar" (or other foods) phrase in their everyday conversation. Some even changed the meaning of What No, to quite rude Meanings.

I have been quite surprised that today how many people can remember Mr Chad very clearly.
Next to food everybody was thinking about new clothes. The men who had been demobbed were given clothes, suit, shoes, and socks, underwear and a couple of shirts. In many cases these were sold, to help with the funds.

Most women and girls were already in some form of savings club. The men decided to do the same, they saved with the local Tailor for suits etc.

They would give him so much each week to save till they had enough monies for what they wanted. When they had paid for the first thing they got they carried on saving for something else. If he did not have what was required, he would order it. Sometimes it would be 8 or 9 months before they were ready. Not because the Tailor did not have time to make them. It was getting the material that took the time.

Everybody had a ration allowance for clothes of 66 coupons a Year.

After being in darkness for years, it was good when the street lighting came on; I had not seen the World lit up. When Neon lights came out it was amazing, you could see things that had always been there, but we had not noticed them before.

All the torches were thrown away. No dark coloured materials up at the windows. The Kelly Lamp was saved for stopping the toilet in the yard from freezing till we got used to it we thought we were in wonderland.

The songs of the day were "When the lights go on again all over The World", there will be peace and laughter and joy ever after "

"Roll out the Barrel we`ll have a barrel of fun."

Not to forget Marlene Dietrich's "Lilly Marlene"

"Underneath the lamp light by the barricade darling I Remember the way you used to Wait"

The electric washing machine came out, no more tubs, mandles, or pounces. (What is a ponce?) It has a round wooded quite thick disk about 12" across, attached to a stail like a brush or a mop. This is used by agitating it up and down in the wash tub with the washing in.

Everyday the Radio gave reports of happenings during the War which were to be revealed to the World?

One such report was the Bombing of Hiroshima and Nagasaki, which were delivered by the USA?
The USA brought in Physicists and Scientist from all over the world. They worked for sometime on the development of the Atom Bomb. They were fully aware what devastation they would cause.

On Aug 6th 1945 the first bomb was dropped on Hiroshima. It killed 95% of the people, who were within half mile of the centre, and many thousands who were farther way. Uninjured people who had died mysteriously in the next few hours and days, became ill, the Doctors did not know if they had died of Radiation or Shock. At first the Doctors thought they were dealing with a new illness. The sickness was in 3 stages:
Stage 1 Bleeding, violent sickness, and sores.
Stage 2 Became ill 10-15 day after the bombing, hair

falling out, Diarrhoea, fever. Twenty to Thirty days later radiation sickness, gums bled, drop in white blood cells, reducing the capacity to fight infection, leaving open wounds.

Stage 3   Instead of the white blood cells coming back to normal they increased much higher, causing many complications. Scars healed with rubbery tissue.

Some patients depending on how much radiation they had received, died within days others dragged on for months. Everybody was crying out for water.

The first time it rained after to bombing the rain was black. Women, Children and men, were stood outside catching black rain water in cups, containers,
Some just stood there with their heads back and mouth open catching the black rain water. It was not know till after, that the mushroom which the explosion caused contained different chemicals beside radio active particles. They went up in the Air with the mushroom. These got into the clouds, which caused the rain to be black, and Radio Active. People were drinking as much water they could get, causing radiation internally. The exact total of deaths is not know it is estimated at two hundred thousand.

The Japanese Emperor Hirohito at the time did not want to end the war. His advisors very strongly advised him to do so.

On 9th Aug 1945 a second Atom Bomb was dropped on Nagasaki. The result was almost identical to Hiroshima. With Seventy Four Thousand deaths.

10th Aug 1945. Japan surrendered.

When reality confronted you with things you could not have anticipated, it was unbelievable. To try and imaging what these people had suffered was inconceivable.

The powers in the USA were at first condemned for their actions by the world.
USA stated that by dropping the bombs they had saved millions and millions from death, and a war that would go on for years.

This question would go on unresolved for years "Was it necessary".

Within days it was announced that Germany would have used Atom Bombs on Japan a few days after the USA. Apparently Germany had been recruiting Physicists and scientist from The USA who were working on the USA development of the Bomb.

Other revelations such as the Ill gotten gains of Hitler. Thousands of pairs of spectacles' were found in the Concentration Camps. In a corner, in another corner, were sets of false teeth, in another. Fur Coats, in boxes were watches, bracelets, and all kinds of jewellery, all confiscated from people before they

were sent to the Gas Chambers, these were all in the thousands.
Under ground a huge box was found with gold teeth in which had been taken out of false teeth, some had been yanked out of corpses when they had been gassed.

Furniture of all descriptions taken from Jewish Homes.

Every country he occupied he plundered their Banks, and took any valuables he could find and had it despatched it to the Reich Bank in Berlin. He had the Gold removed from the Reich Bank in Berlin, to The Hills of Bavaria where many hiding places were prepared to hide the Gold, huge holes were dug and lined with wood to protect the Gold. It is not known how many of these hiding places were prepared.

There was approximately 10 tons. Worth $150 million dollars. This was confiscated from the Banks of every country Hitler Occupied.

Beside these Bank monies, further millions were taken from Jewish families along with their possessions, priceless Works of Art, Jewellery, Stock and Bonds, anything of any value.

The loot was taken by truck from the Reich Bank to the mountains of Bavaria.
When they arrived at their destination, they were

not the only Group who had been there delivering there loot.
The haul that was already there was worth more than had just arrived. This caused confusion, who had taken what; this took a lot of time trying to find out what was what. It was decided to call on the Reich Bank in Berlin where it came from.

To everybody's surprise the Reich Bank provided them with a fully Itemised comprehensive account, giving details of numbers on the Gold Bars and the currency.

The gold was stacked on horses, and taken up a mountain pass

At first the people who lived along side this pass took no notice of them,
because, this pass was quite often used by soldiers for training.

They thought the boxes contained equipment for their training. Because they had been going up and down these paths so long one of the residents recognised one of the soldiers it was realized that all the soldiers on the trek were Officers in the German Army, who were dressed in ordinary soldier's clothes.

Then they became suspicious as to what was going on.

The Americans arrived on the site only 2 days

after all the Loot had been hidden they were trying desperately to find it.

The Americans arrested the soldier who had been recognised by the resident, who turned out to be one of the groups Officers? Who had gone up the mountains to prepare hiding places to take the loot. Eventually he did tell them where one site was. The hiding place was found and all the loot was removed.

The hunt was on for the other hiding places in the mountains. Fortune hunters from all over the world went to Bavaria to search.

By this time various things connected to the loot turned up. Two Bars were found in the Bank of England, and various other countries.

This sent all the fortune hunters in a tizzy, several attempts to find it in the 50 and 60 came to a dead end.

It was thought that the leader of the operation a German Captain, who stayed in Bavaria after the war, and acquired quite a fortune, had something to do with the disappearance of the rest of the loot.
The hiding places are still being looked for today. The mountains are now over grown with Trees weeds and such. Plus there are no bumps and uneven ground to give any indication where the hiding places might be. No one knows where the

hiding places are, everybody who had anything to do with it is now dead.

It had been reported that Hitler and Eva Brawne had committed suicide. This was now in question. It was thought that they had both escaped to Brazil or Argentina.

When The Russian Army occupied Berlin, none of our Allies were there. When they did arrive they were told. The Russian Army had found both Hitler and Brawne outside the Bunker.

They had both been burned by his staff in an attempt to save them from Public scorn. The Russians who found them buried them. This still did not stop the story they had escaped.

It was not until 1991 when the Communist Party was over thrown that the truth was known.

The State Museum Archives in Moscow had a new Director, The Museum was full of State secrets which up to 1991 had been locked away in an underground vault with no entry for anybody on the orders of Stalin.

The new Director opened the archive, what he found confirmed to him that Hitler was dead.

A file was found marked Hitler 1946 to 1947. There was also a black box which held part of a skull with a bullet hole in. The left part of the skull was burned.

Apparently when the Russians found Hitler, they immediately contacted Stalin, he gave instructions that what they found had to be a secret.

He had the two bodies taken to Moscow in secrecy.

There was also a blood stain on the couch where Hitler shot himself. Stalin had a blood sample taken from the couch and the skull, they matched. Or did they?

Stalin ordered complete secrecy of these events "why"

National Service continued after the War. Many joined the regular army serving 5 years, this paid better monies with more prospects. All able-bodied men between 18 and 40 were required to make themselves available for National Service.

Those in reserved occupations like mining, farming, and other industries essential to the war effort were exempt. There was a big demand for coal during the war. And one man in every ten conscripts under the age of 25 were sent down the Pitts.

It continued till the end of 1960 and the upper age limit reduced to 25.

The original time of service went from one year to 18 months then to two years when the Korean War was on, in 1950. Exemptions for reserved occupations continued. The majority of the men went in the Army. These men served alongside the regulars throughout the world. In places like Korea, Palestine, Cyprus and Suez, and countries that had broken away from Britain.

The men who wanted to join a particular service often enlisted before being called up for National Service.

A limited number of men could enter the RAF, then not as pilots.

The Navy was only open to those who served a minimum of three years.

For many it was a chance to get away from home and see the world and live a bit. Others found it an inconvenience stopping them from getting on with their career and studies. For some it gave them the advantage of learning skills like, driving, vehicle maintenance, typing or some other skill to use in later life.

If you were not accepted at the National Service Medical it became a stigma.
Young men were embarrassed, they felt inadequate. Telling their Palls was very difficult.

It is my opinion it is a shame National Service stopped. It gave the young lads a sense of worth, discipline and understanding of life.

Not to forget the Women's Services, the WAAFs, and the Wrens.

I had two Aunty Mauds, one Mums and one Dads. Dads Maud was in the WAAFs. One day she was having dinner with friends in the Canteen. They were complaining to each other about the eyes that were always left in the potatoes. The Duty Officer came up to them and asked, smilingly. Any complaints Airwomen? Yes Sir said Maud... "We do not like the potatoes looking up at us while we are eating" Oh he said smiling as he walked away. Two seconds later he came back still smiling. Report to me he said (again smiling) at 9am in the morning, you,you,you, you and you. The five of them reported to the smiling Sergeant the following morning.

Still smiling he ordered them to follow him. Why is he always smiling Maud thought, they soon found out. There you are girls he said, handing them a small kitchen knife each. He knocked on a wall in the cook house, and what came down the chute. A ton of potatoes that needed eyeing, don't forget girls I want every eye out and report to me when you have done them. When they had finished they rubbed their hands together and thought what a good Job they had done.

They reported back to the office as told. Ok he said, girls I am changing the small knife you have for a larger one. The chiefs want the small ones for a special job. Sir they said we have done them all. No I do not think so, as he took them back to the cook house. Low and behold there was another ton.
We got stuck into them. We then realised that the knives he had changed ours for had no points on them, they were blunt making our job very hard.

Within 10 mins it was all over the Camp, everybody had a good laugh. The girls found out later that the Kitchen Staff had played a part in it. They had filed off the points of the five knives, making it much harder to get the eyes out.
The next time he saw them he said good morning how are you. Fine Sir they said. I have had many meals at Aunty Mauds and you would not find an eye in the potatoes.

In dribs and drabs the children who had been evacuated came Home. I did not know this; There was a family who had 2 Children evacuated. Lucy 5 and Len 3, who lived round the corner. Of course living so near to them I got friendly with Lucy. When they came home Lucy look fine, but Len was drawn and pale. Over some time Lucy told me about her experiences when evacuated. They all arrived at the meeting place with their Best Cloths on, carrying their Gas Masks and other few clothes they had. They were taken to a school hall where there were about 50 children all arriving on other trains. As soon as they arrived they were taken into a small room de-loused, bathed and given a set of old clothes weather they needed them or not. Back to the Hall they went.

They were asked one question" Do you wet the bed." This was the only question they were asked. When this question had been asked of every child, they were more or less put into a line in the middle of the Hall.

In came the people, they started viewing the children and picked who they wanted, looking in hair, teeth, and feet. Lucy told me that all the girls were soon chosen leaving quite a few boys, Len was one. Lucy left with the family who decided they wanted her. Len was crying because Lucy was leaving him.
How ever when Lucy arrived at her new home, the Lady went to see a friend of hers, and told them about Len, there was a young boy in this family, because he Mithered about him coming to them, they went back to the Hall to get him. The family Lucy was with were very nice and she stayed with them all the time she was evacuated.

Most of the children had not seen grass, cows and sheep. It took quite some time to get used to them they were scary at first.

Len had a dreadful time, during his evacuation, he went to 4 different families.
One of the families he went to tied him to a large

cartwheel for 2 days in the Barn. Len died at about 25 26 years of age, he never married. He was a weak boy in stature, and did not fit in anywhere. Also he was quite a sickly boy. In later years Lucy wondering what had really happened to him. She wondered if he had been abused in anyway. He never hinted about it, but Lucy was sure.

Apparently there was Two and a Half million children and 4,000 trains left, from London alone. This did not include children who had gone to live with relatives and companies with overseas branches.

By this time the American forces had their feet well and truly under the table.

The children thought they were like Father Christmas, they had a constant supply of sweets or should I say Candy, chocolate and all kinds of goodies from their PX club, ciggies, nylons, anything they wanted they could get.

The women from about 16 years upwards, had a regular date at the railway station in Manchester, on Saturdays and Sundays, and sometimes during the week days they were there to meet the GIs getting off the trains from Burtonwood. I wish I could change heads with one of these girls for half a day.
I am sure I could tell you some stories after.

Everywhere you went in Manchester the places was full of girls and GIs. There were so many that

Time To Remember

eventually the GIs went further out to the Manchester suburbs.

The girls loved them; their Mothers hated them, even though they were always given presents from the PX. Foods, Coffee, cigarettes, Nylons, chocolate, the GIs had no shortage of anything. Many of the girls ended up being Mums, some went over to the States to get married. A bigger percentage came home, than stayed.

Talking of Nylons I must tell you about the first pair I had. I was still wearing the woollen brown or black socks with my liberty bodice on with rubber suspenders.

Word got around that the stocking man on our local market was having both fully fashioned and fashioned nylons on Saturday. Fashioned was the block on the heal was hairy and The fully fashioned had been trimmed. They were very expensive ,fashioned one shilling and six pence. Fully fashioned two shillings.
I must have a pair, I've only got one shilling where I can get the other shilling from before Saturday?

That week I was very good, without being asked I would do things for Mum and did odd jobs for her.

Ede is saying all the time I was to young to have nylons, from what I can remember I was about 11 or 12. Ede said wait till you are a bit older then use Gravy Browning on your legs like I do it won't cost you anything then. A lot of the older girls used Gravy Browning to colour their legs. Some went as far as drawing a black line up the back, just like Nylons.

With Ede saying all this I thought shut up I am never going to get my other shilling if she keeps on like this. However I got my other shilling despite what Ede said.

Saturday came; Queeney and I went of to the Market, as expected he was there. Unfortunately he had sold out of the fully fashioned, he only had fashioned left. I should have known there was some catch to it, nylons so cheap.

On his counter he had a large box with a notice on. Do not open the packets before you buy no refunds or exchanges. You could either take a packet out of the box yourself, or he would give you one. I took one out of the box so did Queeney. We did not take them out of the packet until we got to the Bus Stop; we were dying to open them. We actually open them on the Bus. Queeneys were Ok. When I opened mine I was so upset I could have cried, I did not want to go home and see Ede.

When I did get home I reluctantly took them out of the packet. They had no shape at the toes, they were just stitched across. The seam was up the front not the back. Ede went mad, I told her about the notice

Time To Remember

on the box, no exchanges she said come on we are going back ill give him no exchanges.
Off she drags me, when we got back he had gone, no trace of him anywhere.
I kept these nylons in my draw till I got married in 1956 I must have lost them when moving home.

Things were changing very quickly, take hairdressing, when I first had my Poodle Cut, it was premed with big hot clamps (like to days bull dog paper clips) These were clamped on to very hot Electric Bars,while the clamps were heating up, your hair would be divided while waiting for the clamps to heat up.
The dividing of the hair was done by using squares of rubber about one and a half inches x one and a half, with a hole in the middle. Your hair was pulled through the hole with some thing like a crocheting needle. The perm solution was put on your hair and a small piece of fine tissue like paper was put on each one. Solid metal rollers were used on each of the squares. By this time the clamps were hot ready for your hair these were taken of the machine one at a time, and clamped onto each roller. Your could hear sizzling on your hair, and the smell was awful. Occasionally you would get burnt on the neck or some times on your head. This was thought of as the hazard of wanting to be beautiful.

Today there would be claims for incompetence and neglect, costing the company thousands of pounds.

You had to wait until the clamps had gone cold. This took between one and a half hours and two hours. They were then taken out and your hair washed with a lot of conditioning cream, then you're Poodle Cut was done. Today the Hot Rollers have gone and replaced with what is called a Cold Perm, no hot clamps much better.

The Salvation Army were very active after the war, they provided a Soup Kitchen for the homeless, most of them were soldiers who came home to no families, and the very poor. Later on in the evening in Manchester near what was called the Shambles. The Salvation Army came round with portable cauldrons, and made soup for those in need. This was just one of their duties.
They provided furniture and many other services.

The Women's Royal Voluntary Service also provided similar to the Salvation Army. They provided meals on wheels service to people in their homes.
Held Luncheon Clubs in most Church Halls. Provided housing accommodation, when possible.
The WRVS carried on with their Meals on Wheels service for many years after the war, this service was carried on by Social Services.They have quite a number of volunteers, and provide shops in most hospitals, not just shops , the volunteers man reception desks and various duties.

Mum and Dad were teetotal, Mum was the secretary of the Local Temperance Society in Broughton.

Time To Remember

This movement had a club "The cadets of temperance" for children 10 to 18 years of age. I spent many happy hours both in the Club Room and any outside trips.

Broughton was an area where lots of Polish People made their homes. Quite a few of these families attended meetings, and joined in the events provided, I made a friend of one of the girls who was older than me. Her Mum came to a few social events, Mum got to know her very well, she was a very nice lady and very good looking and a good figure. My Mum was one of the very few people this lady told her story to. I can not remember her name or which Concentration Camp she was in. For recognition I will call her Vee. Vee was taken out of her home with her Mum, Dad and 2 brothers in the middle of the night. They were taken to a Ghetto in Warsaw, they were there for about 3 or 4 weeks.

About 10 Lorries arrived one day, they were filled out, with most of the people from the Ghetto into these Lorries and were told they were going to be rehoused. They were herded on to trains like cattle, they were not compartments just cattle vans. There were so many people to each van nobody could sit or lie down. There was no food, no toilet, no light and no air.
They were in these vans for 3 days and 4 nights. The only time the train stopped was to give them Bread and a little Water. The door was only opened just enough for them to pass the Food and water through.

When they mentioned the toilet, they pointed to the fields and told them to use there.

The first couple of times the train stopped, people were shot when trying to escape. At one of these stops they were given a large bucket to use as a toilet. The sweat, stench and sickness became unbearable after the first day.
Many died especially the children and elderly. Unfortunately one of the deceased was Vees Mum. They were pleased when they got where they we going, it was just a relief to get off. As they were getting of the train the men and women were separated and the children went with their Mums or Dads, her two brothers went with their Dad.

Individually they were assessed and given instructions where to go.
Because of her good looks and figure she was sent to a particular place in the Camp. As she was going she waved and smiled at her two Brothers and Dad. This was the last time Vee ever saw the three of them. She was soon to find out what she was needed for. To entertain and comfort the German Army. The surroundings she was sent to were quite nice, furnished with everything needed, this was done for the comfort of the soldiers. The women had to make sure they were ready when required, those who did not we removed and not seen again. Vees Head told her to make the most of her situation if she wanted to live. This arrangement went on for 3 years. Any children born in these circumstances

who were not blond, blue eyed and fair skin (Aryan) were taken away and disposed of. When Vee was liberated, herself and 3 girls who had been with her all the time, decided to take the option of coming to England, where she married and had a daughter.

I was not old enough to be told this at the time. Mum told me after quite a long time after.

Chapter Four
NOTABLE EVENTS 1950 TO 2007

North Korea invades South Korea, and the War started.
Petrol rationing ends after 10 years.
Sainsbury's open it`s first self-service store in Croydon.
Andy Pandy appears on British TV.
Frank Sinatra Makes his first sell-out tour in the UK.

Films
Sunset Boulevard.
Annie get your Gun.

Sport
Arsenal beat Liverpool 2-0 in FA cup.

Dad retired at 59 years of age, he had not been well for sometime, he had been diagnosed with Bad Angina, he became very tired. He was not at home long when he decided he would take on an Allotment, Mum was quite pleased at this, he sometimes was like a Bear with a sore head not enough to do? Even though he worked in the shop it was not enough for him. The allotment was quite good it was used a lot during the war. It had been turned over a few times. Making it easier for him to handle. He was quite successful with his Pea Pods, Carrots, Radishes, King Edward Potatoes and flowers, roses mainly.

Of course I was in the Dog House again, when shelling the Peas he had grown, I used to eat half of them. I can hear him now shouting "What the hell am I growing um for"? Oh but they are nice and sweet I love them I would say," Like um Like um" he shouted. I like your Mums Buns but I don't eat um all.

Its ok Edwin don't tell her next time, just give them to me and I will see she does not eat them.

She shouted "You're the same with Jelly by the time you have done eating the squares Instead of having a pint of Jelly were lucky to get half a pint by the time you have finished.

I moaned and groaned.

Shut up she said or I will get the Antifligistine out (think that's how the spell it.)
That will shut you up. Quite often she would threaten me with the Antifligistine   she knew how I hated it. Antifligistine is a drawing poultice applied hot with a piece of lint covering it, I used to complain about

how hot it was, you will have to put up with it if you want that splinter out. It was bought in a tin and looked like putty. The tin without the lid, was put in a pan with water, and boiled till the Antifligistine was hot, this was applied twice a day for 3 or 4 days, morning and night. The splinter could be taken out very easy with tweezers. It was good. I was always getting splinters in my BUM and fingers. After trying to get them out with tweezers, we turned to The Antifligestine, and slap a hot poultice on my BUM. It was very hot at first, when it cooled down the smell was not very nice.

This reminds me of my Dad and his Condi's Crystals in the 1st Aid Box. He suffered with sore throats, there was always Condi's in the house. They looked black very small crystals. A pinch of these were put in a glass and hot water added. The became a very dark purple gargle the hotter you could use it the better for you. Any of us just had to say my throat is a bit sore and you got this gargle. When I got married he sent me a tin of these crystals just in case I got a sore throat.

Dad was also a bit of a Joker; he had a string of jokes. Typical of the World Wars 1 and 2 jokes. Besides telling them to us when customers came in the he would tell them his Jokes.

Two boys about the age of 10 came into the shop and asked for Dad.

Mr, they said we went on Cock Robin Bridge and we did not see any man with 365 noses. Dad laughed, how many noses did the men you saw have. One they said. That's correct Dad said,

What Dad had done was the same he did to me a few years earlier. He had said to them. "If you go and stand on Cockrobin Bridge Early on New Years Eve you will see a man with as many noses as There are in the Year"

They took Dad serious; we think they must have been stood there nearly all morning, looking at all the men.

Another one of his many was.
"If it takes a pound and a half of tripe to make an Elephant a waist coat
What does it take to open a shop".
 Answer to be found on any page after this one.

Just one more.
There was a gourmet who boasted he had eaten everything there was in the world. There was just one thing he had not tried and he could not get it anywhere and that was Poiuy. He had a telephone call one day from one of his palls telling him he had found somewhere to get this Poiuy. It was at a Monks Training School in Tibet, it was given as a treat when they finished their five years training. Good said the gourmet I will enrol. Off he went to

Tibet and enrols. It was a hard slog, no drink, no speaking and scrubbing floors.
At the end of the 5years he could not wait much longer. His hands were red raw with scrubbing, he was dying for a drink. The day came and the Chief went into the dinning room and said. Right lads, your training is over, you can enjoy your last special Meal with us. What do you want Meat Poiuy, Meat and Potato Poiuy or Steak Poiuy.

Mum had a few but they were serious ones.
This one she used to tell me time after time, it took me ages to realise what she meant. "Pam if you only have 3p in your purse and do not owe anything .
You are on your way to being a millionaire".

There were quite a lot of Incendiary Bombs dropped which had not exploded, occasionally one would go off, they did in fact kill a couple of people. Everybody was alerted to these bombs, we were told not to touch them. And phone the Police immediately.

In our school the password "Beatle" was given to all the children, because the School was in an area where a bomb could be hiding. We were told that if we hear anybody shouting Beatle, beetle, we had to go immediately down into the school cellar and not to cause panic.
Plus if you were on your way to the cellar, and saw somebody say to them Beatle, Beatle. We had practise runs so we would know what to do. Who ever thought this up was raving mad it caused mayhem

with the children they were making things up, and pointing to the ground and shouting Beatle if there were any girls about they would go mad.

Baby Boom in 1948, in this year there were more babies born since any year after WW1.
Most of these new Mothers were very young.
People were catching up post War!

The term Baby Boom covered a period from 1948 to 1960.

At the age of 12 it's was my time to be confirmed, at St Georges Church. Before you could be confirmed you had to take a month's class on being able to understand what Conformation was all about.

For a couple of week before the event I had not been well. Pains in my midriff.
The day arrived, dressed all in white, with veil. We arrived at Church. After sitting for a quarter hour we proceeded to walk down the isle carrying our prayer books. The church spun round before my eyes and the pain I had was excruciating. I made it to the alter and the Bishop of Middleton confirmed me.
I thought God was punishing me for something I had done. I had the most awful pains as I turned round to go back down the Isle. I passed out, I remember, the Bishop saying have you seen her eyes. Mum came to me, as soon as she saw me she gasped. My eyes, finger and toe nails were a bright yellow, my

skin just yellow. I had yellow jaundice. Apparently the colour does not come out till after a few weeks of being ill. I just made confirmation, it took several weeks before I got back to School.

Recreation was the utmost thought in the teenager's minds. Sunday morning was like a fashion parade for the Girls. Broad St was the Main road in our area. On Sunday mornings boy and girls would walk from one end of the Street to the other, calling at one of the two Ice Cream shops, the shop most popular was Williams. They had tables and chairs in the shop making it the most popular.

There was good a mixture of boys and girls, many romances were born from these Sunday morning walks.

We stayed there quite a few hours bringing us to Sunday afternoon we would go home have tea then off to the Cinema 10d upstairs and 5d down.
The pictures came in to there own during this time with such Films as:-
Annie Get Your Gun.
African Queen.
Street Named Desire.
I`m Singing in the Rain. (On of my favourites)
Ivanhoe.
Kiss me Kate.
From here to Eternity.

Mrs Williams bought undecorated Easter Eggs. She always wanted somebody to ice the names on. For two consecutive years I earned quite an amount of monies, icing names on Eggs in my spare time.

The American Based at Burtonwood, had found Williams`s, and started to come in regularly, it was here I had my first encounter with GI`s. There was one who drove me mad, no matter what I said I could not get rid of him. At the end one of the boys from our regular Gang took him to one side and told him where to go. It worked because he or his buddies ever came in again.

Notable Events in 1951
King George VI opens The Festival of Britain on the south
Bank of the Thames.
Britain gives USAF permission for airbase
At Greenham Common.

Films
African Queen.
Lavender Hill Mob.
Streetcar named Desire.

Sport
The Oxford boat sinks in the boat race,
A re- run takes place 2days later, Cambridge wins.

Notable Events 1952
King George Vl dies of cancer.
Twenty six people die at the Farnborough air show when a prototype aircraft disintegrates into the crowd.
Foreign Secretary Ernest Bevin states that Britain will build their own nuclear bomb, it is tested on 3rd October 52.
Eva Peron dies in Argentina of cancer age 33.
The Queen makes her first Christmas speech.

Films
Ivanhoe.
Greatest Show on Earth.

Sport
Newcastle beat Arsenal to retain the FA cup.

Notable Events 1953
128 people die when the car ferry Princess Victoria Sailed with her cargo doors open, the boat sank off the Coast of Ireland.
Queen Elizabeth 11 was crowned
The conquest of Everest by Edmund Hillary and Tenzing
Norgay, it is seen as a present for the new young Queen.

Films
Kiss me Kate.
Roman holiday.
From Hear to Eternity.

Sport
Blackpool beat Bolton in the FA cup 3-1

1953 was the year Queen Elizabeth was crowned. We bought our first TV for this occasion. TVs could be rented per week. A slot machine was fixed to the TV, if you wanted to watch something you put either 5p or 6p for 1 hour
Viewing in the slot. About 20million worldwide watched this occasion. Approx 500.000 thousand TVs were bought .

The programme most viewed was the "Test Card" It came on at 10.30pm when broadcasting finished and remained on till 7am next morning.
I do not remember much about the programmes; it is the "Test Card"
That is imprinted in my mind I could draw it no problem. Until we got used to it we would just sit staring at it, in wonder.

When colour came out in the 70s it was spectacular and made all the difference. The Black and White Minstrels were shown once a week, the colour was mesmerising.

Pamela Thompson

Notable Events 1954

It is nine years after the end of the war, rationing was finally over. Housewives and others in our area decided to have a ceremony and burn the Ration books. There were hundreds of them, the fire was as Big as bonfire night.

Roger Bannister ran the 4 minute mile.
At 18 Lester Piggott rode "Never say Die" and became the youngest jockey to win the Derby.
The polio vaccine was developed and tested.

Notable Events in 1955
Ruth Ellis is hanged at Holloway Prison for the murder of her lover she was the last woman to be hung in Britain.
Albert Einstein age 76 and James Dean age 24 die in car crashes.

Films.
Rebel without a cause.   Stared James Dean.
The Dam Busters.

Sport.
Newcastle United beat Manchester City 3-1 in the FA cup.

1955 was a significant year for me.
In 1954 just before Christmas, Jack one of the lads in our Sunday Gang came in William`s with his elder brother Peter who was a regular in the RAF. At first

I did not like Peter he made fun of my white ankle socks. Plus wearing my Teddy Girl Skirt, The boys were also wearing Their Teddy boy Suits. What are Teddy Boys and Girls? During the 1950 The Teddy Boys and Girls were inspired by the Edwardian period of cloths. The title Teddy boys came from the names Edwin and Edward. Both these names were shortened to Ted.
Hench the name "Teddy Boys and Girls". The young men were wearing long drape jackets, usually in dark shades. Sometimes with a velvet collar and pocket flaps. High waisted drainpipe trousers. Their shoes had large chunky crepe soles. (Later known as Brothel Creepers or Beatle crushers)
A white shirt and Slim Jim tie and in some cases a brocade waistcoat. Hair styles. Long moulded greased up hair. The boys had a DA at the back their hair , combed to the centre to a point at the bottom (Known as A Ducks Arse or Bum). At the front a large quiff. Also they had the Boston, the hair was greased straight back and Cut Square across the nape of the neck.

That's just the boys now for the girls. Similar to the boys, drapes complete with a hobble skirt. They added such things as straw boaters, cameo brooches, Coolie hats. Anything from the Edwardian period.

Later they changed to Durndle skirts circular with a lot of material and as full as possible, with a stiff net underskirt to make the skirt really stick out.
An elastic Waspy belt. Which fitted round your

waist, usually worn quite tight, to make your waist look smaller. Bags as big as you could get them. A duster coat. If going out dressed up, a pair of high heels as high as you could walk in and white gloves. If going out casual, flat shoes, and white ankle socks. Hair.
Ponytail and Poodle Cut .

Teddy Gangs.
As with many other groups of people they were portrayed as trouble makers. In the 1960 Teddy Boys became "Rockers" and many Rockers passed themselves off as Teddy Boys. They did this by throwing on a drape coat to gain entry into a dance hall where leather jackets were banned.

In 1970 there was a revival of the Teddy boy fashions.

Peter came out with the gang all over Christmas and New Year. By this time I thought he was great. So much so I went to the station when his leave was over on the 15th January. He was the eldest of 4 children, Jack, David and Pauline. Pete was lucky he was on a Squadron in Egypt, with Transport Command. This gave him the privilege of coming home when there was a flight which was coming home for some special reason. He was listed to be on one flight. At the last minute he was taken off the flight just as he was about to board. This is one flight I knew about. He was very lucky the Flight crashed in Malta, at the Blue Grotto. Everybody was killed.

The only problem was he would get up in the morning. The next thing he was on a flight home, so I never knew when to expect him. Once when he came home, I was working at the cinema. I had a date with somebody else; I was supposed to meet him when I had finished work out side the Cinema. About ten minutes before I had finished one of the usherettes told me Pete had just come home and was waiting outside for me. I was panic stricken I look out the front window and there they both were. I asked Ann to tell Keith on the quiet to meet me round the back. Without letting Pete now, she did this and it worked out fine.

Notable Events 1956
The one pound premium bond was introduced.
The top prize was £1000 pound now it's a million.
Self Service shops were opened in the UK.
Manchester City beat Birmingham 3-1 in the FA Cup.

Peter was due home in March his tour had finished in Egypt. He was posted to Strategic Air Command in Suffolk. He only stayed in Suffolk for a few months the travel to Manchester took to long. Peter had a good friend who came back from Egypt at the same time. He was posted to Stafford Maintenance Unit. Steve's home was in Scotland, because he was to far to go home at weekends, he kindly exchanged posting with Pete.

Pete and I decided to get engaged on the 17th March and get married in September. We encountered quite a few problems. Mum and Dad were not in the best of health, and were both teetotal. Pete's Mum and Dad were both in good health, and they enjoyed a drink. Bella Pete's mum had made enquiries at one of the pubs they went to about using them for the reception, in fact she had booked it. I was not happy at this at all; I knew it would not suit Mum and Dad, in fact I do not think they would have attended the reception.

Taking all these problems into account, we were in The local cinema on Tuesday 12th June we could not tell you to this day what film we went to see, We were to busy talking about our problem. It was decided that we would get married in 4 days time 16th June, Just the four of us Pete, Mike, Joan and I.

It was decided that Pete came to see Mum and Dad on the Wednesday morning, which he did? I did of course tell them my self before he came.

After we had told them, we went straight to the Registry Office, the clerk said if we got the forms back to them by noon it was ok for Saturday. Mum and Dad signed for me and we made it back for noon.

My dress was white with tiny pale green flowers on. My coat was the same shade of green. Pete

Time To Remember

was due back at camp on the Monday morning. We went to Blackpool for 2 days, I bet nobody went on their honeymoon with the best man with them. We did. Peter applied for Married Quarters on camp in Stafford, unfortunately there was a waiting list for accommodation.

However in July the RAF informed us that because of the shortage of accommodation on Camp they had decided to put new Caravans on various sites nearby. Again we were lucky ours was one of four in an orchard in a small hamlet called Hopton Stafford. I loved it there it was so different to living in a town. But when it snowed it snowed, we could get no further that the bridge at the End of the lane. We had Cows and a Turkey come to visit us one night. We were awakened by the Van banging and almost swaying. We got up and looked outside and there were 2 cows and a Turkey. The cow was scratching him self on the side of the van, and the turkey was gaggling away. In the middle of the night Pete was trying to get the cow out. I was scared to death of this turkey I ran back in the van, and watched Pete through the window having a giggle. When he came back in he played hell with me for laughing at him. I was in the Dog House Again.

We bought our first car it was a 1936 Austin 7 Ruby. The one with the wheel on the back, and square looking. It took us backwards and forwards from Stafford till I went back home in September 1957 when I was going to be a Mum.

For the 14 months we lived in Stafford I had 2 Jobs, the first was in a slaughterhouse, I did not last long only about a month. All the parts of the cattle which were not used, was sold to a Glue Factory. The vehicle that came to collect these parts also collected from Vets. This vehicle was high sided with no top. The office I was in was on the 2nd floor near the window,I could see inside the vehicle, it was bad enough going in. It was almost full of dead cats and dogs. Coming out was even worse. All the spare parts from the cattle were piled on top of the dogs and cats. The smell was awful and the sight of it was bad. I decided I could not stand it much longer and left.

My second job was just about ok, it was in Stafford Prison. My job was to monitor the monies and anything that came in for the Prisoners I stayed here till I left when I was going to be a Mum. The only thing I did not like about the Job was every time I left the office I had to have a warden with me, even Going to the loo he would stand outside the door. This got on my nerves, I left. I decided to go back home.

During the War the government kept so many premises empty in all Cities.
They were required for emergency events. There was one of these properties near Mum and Ede. It used to be a large shop. The council had made it into 2 flats a bottom and an upper.

When the war was over these properties went up for sale. Mum bought them.
Pete and I had the bottom one for a few months.

Notable Events 1957
France, Germany, Italy, Belgium, Luxembourg and the Netherlands.
Sign the Treaty of Rome to establish A European Economic Community,
Or The Common Market.
Attempts to decriminalize homosexuality in the UK were rejected.
The Queen made her first television broadcast.
Bill Hayley and the Comets set London Rocking.

Films
Bridge over the River Kwai.
Jail House Rock.
Blue Murder at St Trinians.

The most embarrassing thing that has every happened to me was when I was about 3 weeks away from having my baby. I can not remember why but the car was in for repair. We had to go to Pete's mums on the Bus, It was a Saturday morning 3 weeks before Christmas (my son Gary was born on the 20th December) Pete's Mum lived near the Market which 3 weeks to go before Christmas. The place heaving with people. It was a freezing day and I had thick coat on it had large turn back velvet cuffs and very thick and a pair of thick gloves. Pete had his RAF uniform on, including his great coat.

I was fed up having to buy bigger knickers. Mum said don't buy any more wear these of mine they are almost new. Actually they were just the job for the cold weather, they were proper Bloomers Pink in colour, long legs with
Real elastic at the bottom of the legs and waist. When I put them on they we down to my knees very long and warm. I had a pair of these passion killers on the day we went to Pete's Mums.

We had to stand on the Bus, we were almost there when I felt the elastic in mums nicks snap. I quickly put my had in my pocket fished around to find where my nicks were. I grabbed hold of them in my right hand which had a thick glove on .I did not say anything to Pete. As we were getting of the bus I felt my nicks slip. I did not have hold of them. As I stepped down from the buss I felt them slip round my ankles a big pair of Pink Bloomers. I nudged Pete he saw what had happed, I then jumped out of my nicks, he snatched them up from the ground and tried to stuff them into his great coat pocket which were very shallow. I can see him now trying to stuff these nicks in his pocket, he ended up with these Pink Bloomers dangling out of his pocket. I was sure with all the people around that somebody had seen me.

Our son Gary was born on 20th December 1957. He was 10lb born and quite long, he grew to 6ft like his Dad.

Notable Events 1958
Manchester United "Busby Babes in Plane Crash"
Eight players and eight journalists killed in crash.
Britains first motorway is opened, the 8 mile
Preston by-pass.
Notting Hill Race Riots.

Films
Ice cold in Alex.
Dunkirk
South Pacific

Pete was demobbed after serving 5 years.
Mum gave us the deposit for our first house £100
The sale price was an extravagant £350.
We were bothered about having a mortgage of £250.

At that time when the men were demobbed they were given the choice of keeping their kit and given £20. Or return the kit, and have either a Suit or Jacket and Trousers. Two shirts, underwear and socks. Pete chose to give in his kit.

We had the choice of moving to South Africa with African Airways. We decided to stay in England. Peter went as an Extruding Machine Manager. This was in the department where Colgate Tooth Tubes were made.

Notable Events 1959
The USA sends two monkeys into space as a trial for manned space travel.
Buddy Holly dies in a plane crash
The" Mini "is launched its cost £500 if you wanted one.
It was capable of 70 miles per hour.
Duty free wine and spirits were now allowed for travellers abroad.

The Austin Ruby had to be scrapped; it had done lots of service for us. I cried when they towed it away for scrap. It was 24years old, and had a lot of miles on the clock. Its Big End had gone. It was replaced by the A40, which took us on our first holiday for the 3 of us, we went to Jersey - Gary was 3 years old. Until Gary was about 10 we holidayed between Jersey, Isle of Weight, Isle of Man, Scotland and Wales. I was quite surprised with Jersey, I knew it had been occupied by the Germans, but did not know about The German Underground Hospital, which was built by slave labour, shipped over from Poland and other Countries.
Three quarters of these people died with in 6 months, it was a vast place, built in a mountain which was had been chiselled out of solid rock by hand and pick axes, by the slaves. We went inside it had corridors, and wards some of the notices which the Germans

had put up were still readable. It was very cold, dark, and eerie. You could hear the slaves using their axes. There were various things which were still in place, bowls, medical instruments, buckets and even a bed.

When you got to the end of the excavation, you came to what was meant to be another ward. It was just as the slaves were freed, they just put down the Axes and left. The axes were still there in the half finished Ward. You could see where they had just thrown them.

The Hospital was for wounded Germany soldiers. It was never used for this purpose.

I believe that now they have created flower beds covering all the Tunnels.

The last time we booked for Jersey we had a telegram 3 days before we were due to go, informing us that the Hotel had burned down. We have not been since.

Notable Events 1960
National Service came to an end in Britain.
Princess Margaret marries Armstrong-Jones.

Films.
101 Dalmatians.
G.I Blues

Psycho

Sport.
Wolves won the FA cup against Blackburn Rovers 3-0.

Notable Events 1961
The Russian Yuri Gagarin became the first man in space.
Adolf Eichmann (at last) is tried for holocaust atrocities, and condemned to hang.
Communist Russia erected the wall across Berlin to stop the Exodus of East Germans seeking a new life in the West.
Britain applied for membership in the EEC.

Music.
Wooden Heart

Films
The Birdman of Alcatraz.
El Cid.
West Side Story.

Sport
Tottenham Hotspur Won the double.
Children's Hour is dropped from the BBC Radio

Notable Events 1962
Emergency vaccinations after outbreak of smallpox. In Yorkshire.

Marilyn Monroe found dead in her bed.
Trans Atlantic TV becomes a reality as the Telstar Communications
Satellite in Launched.

Music.
Rock a-hula Baby

Films
Dr No
The Great Escape
Lawrence of Arabia

This year I almost had a big change in my life. I went to an Accountants from the Secretarial Services I worked for, the booking was for 4weeks. He was a keen photographer and entered many photo competitions. First he asked me would I allow Gary to be his child model, I allowed this only in my presence. He then attended another show and asked me to sit for him which I did he won 1st prize. I was given the opportunity to be professional photographers model in the world of photography. I gave this a lot of thought and my answer was no, I did not think this was fair to Pete and Gary. It would have required me working nights and weekends. If I had been single I would have done it without question.

<u>Notable Events in 1963</u>
The Assassination of President J.F. Kennedy in Dallas.

Great Train Robbery nets 2.6 million.
Beatle mania continues to take the UK by storm.

Films
The Greatest Story Ever Told.
The Birds
The Pink Panther

Sport
British heavyweight boxing champion Henry Cooper,
Gives Cassius Clay a fright.
He knocks him down, but had to retire with a badly cut eye.

In 1963 Pate and I decided it was time to change house. We bought a semi-detached in quite a nice area. It was close to Gary's School and handy for busses we lived there for 17 years. This was the very bad winter when every where was frozen from Oct to April.

Peter's friend Steve who changed posting with Pete met his future wife Marie.
The first time I met Marie was in married quarters at RAF Syerston Nottingham where they were living. From the word go we got on like a house on fire. Every year we see each other a least twice. We go to each others houses alternately, and have a good natter.

Notable events 1964.
Twelve gang members of the great train robbery are Sentenced to a total of 307 years.
Mods and Rockers clash at seaside resorts in the UK,
Brighton, Margate, South End and Clacton.

Films
Hard Days Night.
Gold Finger.
Mary Pippins.

Sport
Cassius Clay takes the Heavyweight Championship From Sunny Liston.
Steve moved to Preston with Marie.

We were now settled in our new home, even the gardens were looking good. Dad came down and planted flowers, among them were pinks small versions of Carnations. He came down to tend them once a month.

Notable events 1965
Sir Winston Churchill dies at the age of 90.
Ian Brady and Myra Hindley are charged with the Moors Murders.
The Beatles are awarded the MBEs

Films
Dr Zhivago.

Sport
Liverpool win FA cup beating Leeds United.

Gary is 8 now, he is a good boy never causes us any trouble. Only once when he came home from School with a note from his teacher saying an appointment had been made for Wednesday at 11pm with the headmaster regarding Gary.

His Dad and I were very upset about this, when we asked him what it was about he did not know. After trying to get him to tell us for about an hour, we gave up. I did not sleep that night neither did his Dad. I don't think Gary did either. I took the time off work and went to see the headmaster. I could not believe why he had called us in for such a trivial matter.

"I just want you know that he threw his tomatoes under the table" - I was speechless, he never has liked tomatoes.

I did have quite a few strong words with the Headmaster. I had taken the morning off work. He had Pete and I in a tiz woz and we had not slept. He did sort of apologise and we did not have any more letters from him. Gary really did not know what it was about.

Steve Peters Friend was demobbed from the RAF.

Time To Remember

Notable Events 1966
The Breath –Test is introduced on Britain`s Roads.
One hundred and sixteen children and 28 adults are killed in the mining village of Aberfan Wales when a slag heap collapses and buries the local school.
Sport
England beat Germany 4-2 to win the World Cup.

Notable Events 1967
Israel seizes land from the Arabs in the six day war.
Abortions are legalised.
Homosexual practices are decriminalized.
Donald Campbell dies attempting to break the world water speed limit on Lake Coniston.
Dr Christian Barnard performs the first Heart transplant.

Films
Jungle Book.
Bonnie and Clyde.
The Dirty Dozen.

Sport
Cassius Clay refuses military service and is stripped of his World Heavyweight Boxing Titles.

Notable events 1968
US Senator Bobby Kennedy is assassinated.

Sport
Manchester United wins the European Cup
Beating Benfica 4-1

At home in Avondale I kept seeing a lady who was quite familiar to me walking up and down Avondale. One day I was in the front garden when this lady walked past. She looked at me and I looked at her, both together we said Is that Pam and I said is that Joan. Sure enough we had both seen each other, but could not remember who we were. Joan and I were at the same school, she is just two weeks older that me. Joan said hang on a minute I am just popping home and will be back in a few minutes. With this I went in and put the kettle on for coffee. She came back, in her hand was a wooden coat hanger with my name on. She had kept all these years from when we were at school.

Peter also joined Swinton Park Golf Club.

Andrea (Edes daughter) married Neil, I will miss her. She had always baby sat for me. She is moving to Carlisle with her husband.

Notable Events 1969
On the 21 July Neil Armstrong walks on the moon. Buzz Aldrin and Mike Collins complete the 3 man team.

Films
Hello Dolly.
Butch Cassidy and the Sundance Kid.

Dad died in this year, he had been very ill. He died on the same day and almost the same time as Judy Garland. Mum would not let him go into the Hospital. Ede Mum and I took care of him at home. I had not seen my Dads legs before. I know now why he always had his legs covered. It was quite a shock. His legs were very scared and had knots in them this was caused by the sea and debris in WW1.

We had two strange happenings connected to Dad's death. On the morning of his funeral I went into the bath room and as I opened the door of the bathroom cabinet the tin box with the Condies Crystals in which Dad had given to me shot out of the cabinet which was over the wash basin? At side was the bath. Peter had used the bathroom before me and the sink and bath were still a bit wet and the carpet damp. The Condies hit the sink and the top came off. Condies Crystals turn a bright purple when wet. There were bright purple splatters over the sink, bath and carpet. I did not have time to clear it up; I left it till I came back from the Funeral. We had to have new carpet fitted; the sink and bath were Ok but it took ages to get it all off.

I got dressed ready for the day and decided to have a look round the garden. The pinks Dad had planted some years ago were all dead. They were blooming the day before they had all died - Every one of them.

Notable Events 1970
The Beatles split up in April.
First Jumbo Jet lands at Heathrow in January.

Films
Love Story.
Catch 22

This year we went to the Isle-of-Wight again for our holiday. The Hotel we stayed in had dancing every night, I was in my element, there were a few of us in the party and every night we were dancing, this is when my learning the men's steps became an advantage. There was Pete and one of the men in our group who could not dance, I took the ladies as the man, and everybody had a good time.

Notable Events 1971
Charles Manson and 3 of his family are sentenced to death for the Tate murders.
In Northern Ireland, the first British soldier is killed. The IRA plan to Bomb the British Main Land.
By the autumn the troubles claimed their 100th Victim.
The pound goes and Decimalisation takes it`s place.

Margaret Thatcher then Education Secretary stops free school milk.

Films
A Clockwork Orange.
The French Connection.

Sport
Arsenal wins the League and FA cup double.

Gary was now growing up fast the only problems we had with him was that we never knew where he was. I had been taking him for 18 months by car dropping him off outside the building of the Army Cadets. One night he came home his eyes were like glass, slurring his words and staggering. Pete and I were sure he had been taking drugs and we sent him to bed. Pete decided we should take him to the hospital and so we dragged him out of bed, made him get dressed and quick marched him off to the hospital.

We let him see the Doctor on his own and about an hour later the Doctor came out smiling. Calm down he said he could see we were both worried. He's not been on drugs, all his blood reads is Beer. He told the Doctor he had 4 pints in the pub with his palls. He had been going with his palls every Thursday night after I had dropped him off, for 18 months. He should have been at the Army Cadets.

Apart from this and the tomatoes he has been fine, except going out to play in the Drive with my knickers on his head! I used to put any old clothes in a bag in the pantry as Pete always wanted rags for one job or another. Gary saw me put these nicks in the bag and decided he would have a bit of fun with them and his palls outside. Looking through the window I could see them all having a good laugh at Gary with my nicks. I did not let Gary see me I was having a good laugh also.

Nobody ever saw Gary with out a plaster on his knees. He would be climbing over walls and up trees.

Notable Events 1972
Britain`s miners strike over pay and conditions, resulting in nationwide blackouts.
Britain joins the EEC along with Ireland, Denmark and Norway.

Films
The Godfather.

Sport.
Rangers win the European Cup Winner`s Cup Beating Moscow Dynamo 3-0

Mum died this year, she had a heart attack and died in hospital. I think she could not get over losing Dad.

Pete, Eddie (Joan's Husband) Joan and I went on holiday to Isle of Wight to the same dancing hotel. Eddie could not dance either the lads just sat out.
I had been mithering Pete to learn to dance for 2 years but it just fell on deaf ears.

Notable Events 1973
In the Middle East the Yom Kippur war between Israel and Egypt cuts of oil supplies to the UK.
Edward Heath brought in the 3 day working week due to Coal strikes and high price of oil.
Jeans became a must have.

Films
Live and let Die.
Jesus Christ Superstar.
The Sting.

Sport
By beating Leeds, Sunderland became the first second-division team to win the FA cup in 42 years.

I had a shock one day when I got home from work. Pete said how long will it take you to get ready? What for I asked? There is a beginners dance class starting at the Court in Eccles at 7-30. I have never got ready as quick in my life, all night I was thinking he will not come next week. Within a year he had the dancing bug more than I did. We made some good friends, and looked forward to going every week. We had one big problem; he used to go mad at me leading, with being tall I was used to being the gent, it was hard for me to follow.

This was the year that I went to Social Services for 6 week to do the wages, I stayed 21years. I got on very well with Mrs Sweeney who was my Boss, her title was Head of Community Care.

The WRVS was giving up the Meals on Wheels Service the following year and Social Services were taking it over. Mrs Sweeney asked me to stay, and sort out what was needed for the take over, besides taking over the existing rounds they were being added to, this meant all the rounds had to be re jigged. Also we started evening meals. I was only responsible to myself and in sole charge of all Meals on Wheels and luncheon clubs.

Notable Events 1974
Threatened with impeachment President Nixon resigns over Watergate.
Two Birmingham Pubs are bombed by the IRA.
The DC-10 Air disaster killing 344 passengers outside Paris.
A Japanese soldier walks out of the Philippine jungle and gave himself up – no one told him that the war ended 19 years before.

Films
Murder on the Orient Express.

The Man with the Golden Gun.

Sport
John Conteh becomes the first British light-heavyweight World champion for 25 years

Notable Events 1975
Margaret Thatcher is elected leader of the Tories. She is the first female leader of a British political party.
In June the first oil from the North Sea was brought ashore in Scotland. Later in the year the Queen opens a North Sea pipeline.
It was estimated that over 6.5million trees had been killed by Dutch elm disease.

Films
Jaws.
One Flew Over the Cuckoo`s nest.

Notable Events 1976
Prime Minister Harold Wilson resigns after 13years service.
The first commercial flight of Concord takes place from London to Paris.
Britain's hottest summer for 200 years, water is rationed and forest fires sweep the Country.

Films
The Omen.

Sport
Lester Piggott wins the Derby for the 7th time.
At the age of 20, Bjorn Borg became the youngest Wimbledon tennis champion for 45 years.

Notable Events 1977
In the Canary Islands two jumbo jets collided, killing 574 .
Street parties were held throughout the country to celebrate the Queens Silver Jubilee.
Elvis Presley is found dead at his home Graceland's. A drug overdose was suspected.
Charlie Chaplin dies at the age of 88.

Films
Saturday Night Fever.
Star Wars.

Sport.
Red Rum becomes the first horse to win the Grand National three times.
Liverpool wins the European Cup in Rome and the League Championship, but loses The FA Cup Final to Manchester United.

This year was the start of my health problems. To cut a very long story short, my Gall Bladder rotted. The rot went along my Gall tract to my pancreas. The result was as though my pancreas had been pickled in acid. The surgeon cleaned my pancreas as much as possible. The rest of the gung should have been cleared by my body as normal. In 4 months time I had to have another operation. The badness secreted on my pancreas should have gone through my system normally. It did not it. The badness had caused a pseudo cyst on the head of my pancreas.

The damage to the pancreas caused me to become Diabetic. Since I had the last operation I have to take pancreatic enzymes every time I eat, even one biscuit.

Notable Events1978
In Guyana 913 members of the cult The People`s Temple commit mass suicide using cyanide.
Louise Brown, the world's first test tube baby is born in Manchester.
In the winter of "Discontent" a number of trade unions go on strike.

Films
Superman
Grease

Sport
Argentina beat Holland 3-1 in the World Cup.
Bjorn wins his third successive Wimbledon title.
Daly Thompson wins gold in the decathlon at the Commonwealth games.

This was the year Pete and I were asked to go on

the staff at the dancing school, we were expected to dance with the members who were learning and dance with them when they took their tests, this was quite a challenge for us, we would dance with about 24 each people from 9-30 to 3-4pm. When it was a Latin test by the end of the day you did not know if it was Cha Cha Cha, or Rumba the steps for these two dances are similar, the timing is different. We had no problem on Modern tests.

It is quite true when people say I don`t know which is left and right. Over the years this appertained too many. We had one lady, who got so frustrated with herself, she got some cardboard and put L on one and R one the other and she tied them to her shoes on the top, this helped her a lot.

We enjoyed this and carried on till about 84. We had finished our medals in Modern and Latin Dancing, and in the middle of our gold bars. We were with IDTA the International Dance Teaching Association.

While we were there I organised holidays in Europe, only for a week that was long enough. The smallest group was 25 the biggest 42. A week was long enough.

Gary was also 21 and worked as a Motor Mechanic. He had done a 5 year course in mechanics.

Notable Events in 1979

Across the UK rubbish piles build up as the strike continues.
An IRA bomb kills MP Airey Neave as he leaves the House of Commons car park.
Lord Mountbatten is also killed by an IRA bomb.

Films
Monty Python's Life of Brian.
Apocalypse Now.

Sport
Nottingham Forrest wins European Cup.
Sebastian Coe sets new world record for the 800m the mile, and 1500m.

Pete and I were on the move again. We did not have a garage at Avondale and decided to move. We moved to a detached house with much more room.
In the 1st year we pulled it to pieces and almost re-built it. We had a double garage and enough room for 8 cars on the path. We stayed here for 24 years.

Notable Events 1980
North Sea platform collapses.
John Lennon is shot dead.
Breakfast TV given the OK.

Sport
Britain going to Moscow Olympics.

Ted died at 61 he had not been ill so this came as a shock.

Gary suddenly took an interest; he joined the teenagers dance night. This is where he met Alison. After about a year he was doing the stage at the Dancing School he also went to other branches of the IDTA.

This started him off with discos. He still does this today, he has one permanent booking at a local club on Wednesday nights, with his knowledge of music he gained at the school he has done very well with his discos.
He knows what to play if a waltz is requested and understands what to play for what.

Notable Events 1981
Thatcher gives in to miners.
Chapman pleads guilty to John Lennon murder.
Prince Charles and Diana marry.
Mystery disease kills homosexuals.

We had some friends on the Town Twinning. Salford and Lunen in Germany.
We were asked to take the group of teenagers on the annual trip. At first I was not sure about Germany, the only contact we had with them was on holiday when they throw everybody's towels in the pool or sea and put theirs on the sun beds to keep them. You would look through the window at 6.30 in the

morning and there they were putting their towels on the beds to reserve them.

We took the 1982 trip, and found the German family we stayed with were very nice. We had a good holiday.

The bookings for these exchanges were always done by the same travel company. We received our details from them; there was 1 document ticket for all who were going, in our case it was for 25 people.

The night before we were coming home we had a big party. There were only two of the teenagers who were not old enough to drink. Everybody except these two was suffering a hang over and miserable because most of them had found boy or girl friends.

However the coach came to take us to the airport, the friends the group made came to see us off, the girls were crying, they were in a right state.

We got to the Airport, looked on the board for our flight and could not find it.
One of our teenagers was studying German she came with me to the desk and after a lot of messing about we found that the company who made all the arrangements had used the winter time table, there was no such flight in the summer.

The time was 1.30 pm and arrangements were made for us to catch the 8pm flight - but only to London.

Then by shuttle from London to Manchester. The worst was keeping the group together. When it was all sorted out, we were told the flight was going from the far end of the Airport. I asked if our entire luggage be checked in. The answer was a definite NO.

We split the group into 4. We put the most sensible in charge one to each group. We got 4 trolleys and stacked them with the entire luggage. Some of them looked quite unwell it was the effects of the night before.

There were cases falling off trolleys and bags bursting when we were on the way to the far side of the Airport. One of the group leaders was sick. By this time everybody was getting hungry, and nobody had any monies. Pete and I sorted it out they all got a drink and something to eat.

By this time we were tipped off that one of the lad's age 16 had a case and bag full of cigarettes and wine. During our investigation we found nearly all the boys had over their allocations for cigs and spirits. This sent me into a Flap; I thought Peter would bust a gut.

We at last arrived in London. After some thought I decided that before we all arrived at customs. We would pile all the baggage on two trolleys. I would go on a head and have a word with customs and explain what had happened during the day. All

the bags were piled on top of each other. I saw the custom man and explained, I also said that all the cases were coming on two trolleys.
Some were held together with string and we had no idea which case was whose. If he stopped one he would have to stop us all. The cases arrived and we were all waved through, without a word, we had made it home.

The boy we had been told about had 20 cartons of cigarettes and a few bottles of spirits he was only 16. The other boys did not do too badly, not as much as Tim, but enough.

Notable Events 1982
Laker Airways goes bust.
Argentina invades the Faulklands. 2nd April.
Marines land in South Georgia.
RAF bombs Port Stanley.
British submarine sinks Argentina cruiser.
Argentines destroy HMS Sheffield.
Ceasefire agreed in Falklands on 14th June.
Princess Diana has Prince William.
Queen fends off bedroom intruder.
In Australia the Mother of the baby taken by a Dingo, is jailed.

By this time I was ready for a change of work and I fancied work out in the community. I applied for the post of Relief Day Care, Officer in Charge. I managed to get this post and enjoyed every minute of it. My position called for me to have keys for all the centres.

One November at about 10.30 pm I was up stairs at home when I heard an explosion. Just as I looked out of the window there was another bang we lived on a hill overlooking everything at the back, I saw the smoke bellowing from the Broughton area. The Local Chemical works had blown up.

After some consideration of the time, I decided to telephone our Director at home. He had just gone to bed and had no idea what had happened. He gave me the entire job of going to our nearest centre and do what ever was needed. I phoned the Police and told them I was on my way and I also phoned our transport manager, to send the Social Services vans and be ready in case the mattresses were needed. When I arrived at the site it was just like a war zone. People and children stressed.

Just as the mattresses were being delivered the Police came to tell us we had to get out, there was chance that chemical fumes were coming our way. By this time 3 Social Services busses arrived. We all went to Lime Court. Lime Court had an elderly person home next to it and most of the staff came over to help. At the home they had plenty powdered soup and I phoned the local bakery and they gave us all the bread that had not sold during the day.

Pete the Director and Deputy Director came to see

if I needed any help. By this time it was 9am the following day and he insisted I went home, this was after I fell a sleep at the Desk.

Gary and Alison were married in September. I like Alison very much and I have told her on many occasions that I can not think of anybody better who I would rather have looking after my grandson.

Edes Harry died at the age of 59 with Cancer. Ede was still working; this I think helped her to get over him. They were both the same age.

Notable Events 1983
Britain wakes up to morning TV.
Seat Belts to be worn.
Police hunt Shergar's kidnappers.

Sport
England fans rampage in Luxembourg.

Notable Events 1984
Michael Jackson gets burned when doing Pepsi Advert.
Torville and Dean win Olympic Gold.
Miners Strike over pit closures.
Scientists find Aids virus.
Moscow pulls out of US Olympics.
Pound notes go, now we have a pound coin.

Pamela Thompson

Notable Events 1985
Miners call off year long strike.
English teams banned after Heysel.
UAFA bans English clubs from Europe.
Live Aid raises millions for Africa.
Titanic wreck captured on film.

Sport
Fans killed in Bradford Stadium fire.
Fans die in Heysel rioting.
Europe wins Ryder Cup.

Pete's Mum died in hospital

Notable Events in 1986
Greater London Council was abolished.
Prince Andrew and Sarah Ferguson marry.
UK oldest twins turn 100.
Police renew hunt for Moors victims

Notable Events 1987
Police crack down on soccer hooligans.
Ian Brady the Moors Murderer helps to search for Moors victims. Ian Brady claims more killings.
Liverpool fans to stand trial in Belgium.
Lester Piggott jailed for three years.
King's Cross Station fire kills 27.

Notable Events 1988

Piper Alpha oil rig ablaze.
Egg industry fury over salmonella claim made by Edwina Curry.
Jumbo jet crashes onto Lockerbie.
First clue to Lockerbie crash found.

Gary and Alison have been married now for six years and I had given up any chance of having grand children. The day they came and told us Alison was going to be a Mum I was jumping up and down, singing, dancing and laughing, crying at the same time. I was thrilled to bits. Andrew arrived on the 9th April 1988.

We also went to see David, Pete's Brother in Australia, and Perth for the first time we were a bit nervous the Lockerbie Air crash had just happened 3 days before we were going.

Notable Events 1989
Football fans crushed at Hillsborough
Yorkshire Ripper's wife wins damages.
Massacre in Tiananmen Square China.
Britain's oldest person turns 112.

Notable Events 1990
Freedom for Nelson Mandela.
Rioting inmates take over Strangeways Prison Manchester.
Three countries lift beef export ban, from Britain

One in five British yet to pay poll tax.
Thatcher quits as prime minister.
Tories choose Major for No 10.

Notable Events in 1991
US Congress votes for war in Iraq.
Mother of all Battles` begins`.
Bush threatens Iraq with land war
US bombers strike civilians in Bagdad
Pavarotti sings in the British rain
Maxwell Business Empire faces bankruptcy

Notable Events in 1992
US stops breast implants.
Fergie and Andrew split up.
Controversial Diana book published.
Church of England votes for women priests.
Queen to be taxed from next year.
Bomb explosions in Manchester.
Windsor Castle on fire.
Queen`s Christmas speech leaked.

Joan and I had a holiday just the two of us we went by coach to Italy Lake Como. While we were there Pete's Dad died.

Notable Events 1993
Jamie Bulger 2 years old found dead. Two boys charged with the toddler`s murder.
Child killed in Warrington IRA bomb attack.

USA Waco cult siege ends with inferno.
Michael Jackson accused of child abuse.

Joan and I went to Bulgaria for a week, I had been there quite a few times but Joan had not. She was quite surprised.

Notable Events 1994
Guilford Four cleared of IRA murder.
Mandela becomes SA`s first black president.
Camelot wins UK lottery race.
Sunday trading legalised.
Britain's first lottery draw.
Norway votes no to Europe.
Race ace Senna killed in car crash.

Eddie, Joan's husband, died he had been ill for a long time.

Also Joan had a very bad accident she broke her arm in a fall, the break has still not grown any bone, which has limited her in many ways. She stayed with me for a few weeks when she came out of Hospital I did not want her to be on her own.

Notable Events 1995
Fred West serial killer found hanged, by his own hand.
Eric Cantona banned over attack on fan.

First man jailed for male rape.
Ecstasy pill put party girl in coma.
Diana admits adultery in TV interview.
Rosemary West gets Life sentence.
Charles and Diana divorced.

Peter was Captain of the golf club in 94-95. I tried playing just for him, I am afraid that I did not do very well; I have never been a walker. Trouti , the wife of one of Pete's friends was also learning - we played together. I loved going round the course it is so nice - streams, lake trees etc. I always had my butties and a flask in my golf bag. Trouti also had the same. There were four trees on the course which had been sawn down which made good tables. When we got to them we would stop, have a buttie and coffee and a cig. (A key) Until somebody in the club complained about us, they claimed we were holding them up. (Me in trouble again) We gave up after that, golf was spoiling our walk about.

Pete and I enjoyed his year as Captain. We had never eaten so much, all the dinners we went to- 3 and 4 a week sometimes. Bouquet presentations, it was a very busy time. We also enjoyed his following year as Ex Captain, not as time consuming but nice.

Notable Events 1996
Massacre in Dubliner school gym.
Huge IRA explosion rocks central Manchester.

Handguns to be banned in the UK.

Notable Events 1997
Princess Diana starts landmine row.
Widow is allowed to have dead husband's baby.
Dolly the sheep is cloned.
Princess Diana dies in Paris car crash.
Diana's funeral watched by millions
Great Train robber escapes extradition.
Tiger Woods wins The Masters age 21.

When Alison and Gary got married in 82, she decided to get married, instead of continuing her education. At the age of 37 she decided to go to University and carry on with her Degree in Biology. I was quite concerned at this, looking after a house and looking after Andrew I hoped it would not be too much for her. Pete and I along with Bill and Jenney (Alison's Mum and Dad) looked after Andrew. I love Alison I look at her as the daughter I never had. I used to love it when we went out for lunch, just Alison, Andrew and I.

Notable Events 1998
President Clinton denies affair with intern.
Linton admits Lewinsky affair.
The real IRA announces ceasefire.

Joan married again to Allen; I was so pleased for her.

She sold her home in Avondale and moved in with Allan. She was only just round the corner from me. We started playing Scrabble about this time, and we are still playing at my home on Tuesdays. When she came this Tuesday she was peeping over my shoulder trying to see if I was writing about her.

Andrew our grandson was 10 this year. Gary, Alison, Pete and I took him to Disney Land. A good time was had by all.

At ten minutes to twelve on New Years Eve of this year I had 2 heart attacks one after the other. Followed by 2 angioplasties during the year. That kept me quiet for a while.

Notable Events 1999
Britain gets first minimum wage.
Dozens hurt in London bomb blast.
Millions marvel at total eclipse
Olympic officials face bribery changes.

We spent the Millennium with Joan and Allan at the Golf Club.

Notable Events 2000
The World celebrates the Millennium.
Life for serial killer Dr. Shipman.
Ford quits Dagenham after 70years.
Blair's` 4th child in born.

Time To Remember

<u>British pioneers develop HIV vaccine.</u>
<u>Concord crash kills 113.</u>
<u>Ministers misled public on BSE.</u>
<u>Schoolboy Damilola Taylor dies of stabbing.</u>

Alison graduated this year; she attained a Masters Degree in Biology. Peter and I would have loved to see her graduate but of course her Mum and Dad came first. I was so proud of her in her cap and gown, it is a lovely photograph. She is doing extremely well; she is Head of the Biology at a university.

We made our second trip to Florida with Gary, Alison and Andrew. The first time we went we only saw Disneyland, Sea World and Animal World. This time we wanted to see Bush Gardens and Daytona Beach. We also spent 4 days at Grand Bahamas, and swam with the Dolphins.

<u>Notable Events 2001</u>
Dr Harold Shipman my have killed hundreds`
James Bulger killers win anonymity for life and are released.
Foot and mouth scar at UK abattoir.
Donald Campbell's speedboat is recovered from Lake Coniston.
Big rise in new cases of foot and mouth.
Crisis as foot and mouth spreads.
Healthy cattle to die to save Exmoor.
Diana butler to be charged with theft.

30,000 postal jobs to be cut.

Unfortunately Pete was taken very ill, after being so fit all his life, it was terrible to see him go from 6ft to 5and a half feet and from 13st to 9 and a half stone. He eventually straightened up and got his weight back. God pulled us through the most horrible time in our lives.

Notable Events 2002
UK now free of Foot and mouth.
Woman granted right to die.
Queen Mother dies.
Diana Ross arrested for drink-driving.

Notable Events 2003
US launch missiles against Saddam.
Saddam's sons killed in battle.
Saddam's statue topples with regime.
Jonny Cash dies.
End of Concorde era.
Bon Hope dies.
England wins Rugby World Cup.
Saddam Hussein is captured.
Ian Huntley found guilty of Soham murders.

Considering what had happened to Pete in 2001 and the problems I have, we decided to move. It took us a long time to find what we wanted but eventually we found an Apartment in a Conservation Area. It has a large lounge, 2 bathrooms, and 2 large Bedrooms. Just what we wanted - especially 2 bathrooms. We are in a block of 6 apartments, no gardening, and no looking after gardens and no window cleaning. The building maintenance is also taken care of. It is all taken care of out of our monthly charge for up keep of the building.

Notable Events 2004
Dr Harold Shipman hangs him self.
Dads who are angry through purple flour at Toni Blair.
Yasser Arafat dies.
Thousands die in Asian tsunami.

Notable Events 2005
Charles and Camilla to be married.
Ban on Hunting comes into force.
Charles marries Camilla.
IRA declares end to arms struggle
England wins the Ashes.
Pubs open 24 hours.
London to host 2012 Olympics.

05 has been a very sad year. Ede was diagnosed with Altzimers. She does not know where she is and does not know who she is. She refers to Andrea (Edes) daughter as that woman and she thinks I am Andrea.

All her married life Andrea has lived away first at Carlisle then Worstershire.
We only see her couple of times a year.

Notable Events 2006

Pete and I celebrated our Golden Wedding - 50 years. You don't get that for murder these days! I do not know how we made it; we have always fallen out and argued. To be very honest when people tell me they don't fall out, I think the opposite. I can not see when two people live together and do not argue.
It must be a dull life.

Over the years we have taken to cruising for our holidays we have been very lucky there are not many places in the world that we have not seen. The two cruises we had in this year, ended in disaster for me. Pete and I went on a Caribbean Cruse again in January. This particular day we had booked our trip for 1.30pm in the afternoon, we had the morning free. We were in Antigua, and decided we would go for a walk on shore. On our way back to the ship, I fell don't ask me how I fell - I don't know, but I had broken my wrist in 2 places. This was not the worst disaster.

We had our second trip on the Oriana; it was our 50th anniversary on the 16th June. Joan, Allan, Pete and I went on the Top of The World cruise.

When we got to the Coach to take us to Southampton, a friend of Pets from the Golf Club Jim and his girlfriend Helen was already there, they joined in our 50th celebrations.
Pete and I are going to their wedding in September.

When we got on board arrangements were made to renew our vows on Friday 16th by the captain of the Oriana. On Wednesday the 14th Joan and I were going to a computer class on board. The arrangements were I was to meet Joan in the class. Pete and I had been sat on the deck and as I got up to go to Joan, I was a bit late so I hurried. I saw this sun bed on the deck sticking out and what did I do - Fell over it. I landed face down on the deck and busted my left eyebrow.

Everybody was trying to help it looked as though I was bleeding to death, sos`s were sent out all over, within 2 mins there were 2 Doctors and 3 nurses with me, they were concerned about blood loss until I told them I was on blood thinners for my heart. Panic over I thought but no the next thing they were closing the deck and another lady Dr Came. They took me away up to the medical deck on a stretcher and put 5 stitches in my left eyebrow the lady Dr stitched it for me and did a good job. There is not a mark on my eye where she had stitched it.
Joan told me later that when she got to the computer

class the Dr who stitched my eye was taking the lesson also. It came over her phone as a code 1 emergency and come quickly they had a patient bleeding badly on The Port Side. Joan told me that she ran out as though her tail was on fire. Joan did not think for one minute it was me.

The next morning Thursday I had to go to see the Doctor, I had no idea how she knew. She said to me I believe you are getting married again by the Captain on Friday. She then said. What will happen in the morning when you go to the hairdresser the make-up artist will come and he will camouflage your eye, hoping it's not too bad for the afternoon. I started to cry I thought it was such a nice gesture. He did a very good job considering I had 5 stitches in it.

The experience of getting married again is very moving, I was ok up to where the Captain said do you take Peter - At that very moment I busted out in tears again. Joan gave me 2 hankies then I was ok again.

The reason Joan and I were on this cruise was because we both wanted to see the Snow Cap and the Rising Sun. The weather was so bad both these events were cancelled by the Captain. We were talking to a man who was on 7th trip to see the Snow cap and the Rising Sun. That was it for him; he said he was giving up trying.

We booked the Golf Club for family and friends to celebrate our 50th

David (Peters younger Brother) was coming to stay with us for 4 weeks on the 27th July from Australia. Sadly Kath David's wife died earlier this year.

We arranged the celebration at the Golf Club for the last Sunday in July, enabling David to join us.

We enjoyed having our family's and friends around. Joanne my hairdresser and Michelle my Home Help came to the party, they have been coming to me for quite a few years. I have become very fond of them both they are more like family than a hairdresser and home help.

Notable Events 2007
This year in June we were cruising in the Greek Islands, Turkey and Cyprus.

I was not with Pete as he had to dash back to the boat and I was walking along on my own, when a laidened trolley came up behind me and ran over my left foot at the side. It was one of those trolleys which have a double wheel. The lady was pushing it and I was trying to get my foot out, what she did was push the trolley forwards, when it should have been backwards. I ended up on the ground on my left knee which took a chunk of skin from my knee. By the evening it was another visit to the ships hospital. It's a good job we were covered by insurance; the three accidents cost over £1000 pounds.

In September we are going on a cruise round the British Isle`s and France. I am keeping all my fingers and toes crossed hoping I will not have another mishap.

My Grandson who I completely ruin has grown to be taller than both his Dad and Granddad, he is six feet 3 inches and has all the girls chasing him - he is very good looking. He is now 19 and finished College in May. He has a place in University for 2008. He has decided to have a gap year which the university have agreed to. His ambition is to become a Drama and Arts Teacher.

For the past 5 years he has saved every penny he has been given and saved the wages he has earned and has just bought his self a new Ford Fiesta.

It has taken Gary just over a year to build a double conservatory; downstairs shower room, toilet, and utility room and extend a bedroom. He has done this and his job at the same time. The only thing he has not done is the bricklaying and plastering. He has done a good job.

Alison is still teaching. It is their Silver Wedding in September - 25years. They are off to Florida to celebrate.

Ede still lives in her house and will not move and insists she is not ill. David (Edes son), David's wife Helen, myself and Andrea when she can get down. She has a daughter Claire who is married. We all look after her in her home.
We did arranged a carer for her, when they arrived she would tell them they were wasting their time, there is nothing wrong with her and would not let them in. Altzimers is a very upsetting illness, the sufferer does not remember anything at all, and is quite happy, in a world of their own. For the carer it is very upsetting seeing someone who you love, I am not nasty when I say this my sister is not my sister any more, she has no idea of time or place. When I am ready to take her out I ring her, she answers. As soon as the phone goes down she forgets I have been speaking to her. I get to her house let myself in, the first thing she says Hello where have you been I have not seen you for months? Come on Ede the Car is waiting for you outside. You have got no Car she says. I have had a Car for years and years.

When I take her home and we get in her drive she won't get out of the Car, she says she has never seen this place before. One most upsetting thing she has said to me was when she asked me if she had been married and does she have any children. David goes to see her every night, I see her a few times a week. And take her out on Saturdays.

Helen (David's wife) is very good to her she takes her

washing home and brings it back washed and Ironed, gets her pension, does her shopping and cooks for her. David has a daughter and two granddaughters. I feel sorry for them she will not let them in sometimes. Ede has for some reason taken a dislike to 3year old Selby. She makes her cry when she sees her I could not believe this until I saw it for myself. I have told them not to take her again.

Since retirement I have plenty of "Time to Remember". I have enjoyed writing this book, if anybody would have told me I would write a book, I would have not believed them. It is amazing what comes to mind when you sit down and think.

They say everybody has at least one book in them, it must be true.

Peter and I keep taking our tablets and falling out, and are still here.

ABOUT THE AUTHOR.

I have no credentials as an Author, only life experiences from 1937 to 2007
These stories are true events and stories of real people pre-war, during the war and post-war.
Some are very sad, and some amusing, all are true accounts.
My family and friends are also included in this book, especially the last third.
They say that everybody has a book in them waiting to be written, from my perspective this is true. This is my first book, if anyone had told me six months ago I would write a book I would have thought they were crackers.
At the age of 70 you would expect somebody to write their last book not the first. If you are reading this and you fancy writing your first book have
A go. It keeps your brain alive and things that have been stored in the recesses of your mind come back to you very clear. I have enjoyed writing this book, I'm not to sure my hubby has, to many late meals, a lot of shushes, and I wont be a minute.
OH and one more thing get your self an understanding publisher like I have.

Printed in the United Kingdom
by Lightning Source UK Ltd.
126639UK00001BB/265-267/A